Barcley Toys Transports & Cars

1932 - 1971

I0792548

Howard W. Melton
and
Robert E. Wagner

Schiffer Publishing Ltd
4880 Lower Valley Road, Atglen, PA 19310 USA

Library of Congress Cataloging-in-Publication Data

Melton, Howard W.
Barclay toys : transports & cars, 1932-1971 / by Howard W. Melton and Robert E. Wagner.
p. cm.
ISBN 0-7643-2127-7 (pbk.)
1. Automobiles—Models—Collectors and collecting. 2. Automobiles—Models—Catalogs. 3. Barclay Manufacturing Company of New Jersey. I. Wagner, Robert E. II. Title.
TL237.2.M45 2004
629.22'12'075—dc22
2004011730

Designed by Mark David Bowyer
Type set in Tango BT/Souvenir Lt BT

ISBN: 0-7643-2127-7
Printed in China

Published by Schiffer Publishing Ltd.
4880 Lower Valley Road
Atglen, PA 19310
Phone: (610) 593-1777; Fax: (610) 593-2002
E-mail: Info@schifferbooks.com

For the largest selection of fine reference books on this and related subjects, please visit our web site at
www.schifferbooks.com
We are always looking for people to write books on new and related subjects. If you have an idea for a book please contact us at the above address.

This book may be purchased from the publisher.
Include $3.95 for shipping.
Please try your bookstore first.
You may write for a free catalog.

In Europe, Schiffer books are distributed by
Bushwood Books
6 Marksbury Ave.
Kew Gardens
Surrey TW9 4JF England
Phone: 44 (0) 20 8392-8585; Fax: 44 (0) 20 8392-9876
E-mail: info@bushwoodbooks.co.uk
Free postage in the U.K., Europe; air mail at cost.

Dedication

Howard W. Melton wishes to dedicate this book to his wife, Jo Anne Melton, and his children, Heather and Patrick. Robert E. Wagner wishes to dedicate this book to his wife, Alice; his sons, Bob, Don, and Jeff; and his grandchildren, D.J., Theresa, Ryan, Tyler, and Jake. Jo Anne and Alice deserve special note, for not only did they encourage the authors as they researched, wrote, and edited this volume, but also tolerated many late night telephone calls as Howard and Robert compared notes, exchanged ideas, and discussed newly discovered information.

Acknowledgments

The authors wish to thank Jennie Rakos, Jo Anne Melton, and Bill Lango for their very careful reading and editing of the text and their many helpful comments. We would like to thank the many people that we talked to while gathering information for the book including John Schutz, Myron Shure, Richard O'Brien, Robert E. Turnquist, James Ramaley, Marv Silverstein, and Stan Alekna. We are particularly appreciative of the help of Bill Lango who both provided us with information about the Barclay Manufacturing Company and with suggestions as to others to whom we might speak to gather additional information. We also wish to acknowledge the encouragement and assistance of our editor, Doug Congdon-Martin, Peter Schiffer, and all of the employees of Schiffer Publishing, who assisted us with this project. The examples shown in the photographs are from the collections of the authors.

Photographic & Website Credits

Barry Rustin, a professional photographer specializing in architectural, portrait, and product photography, spent many hours taking the wonderful pictures that are included in the book. We both acknowledge and thank him for his efforts and professionalism. Barry's business is Barry Rustin Photography, Evanston, Illinois.

The accompanying Website was designed by Jeff Westover. We both appreciate Jeff's professional approach to this project as well as his many excellent suggestions and recommendations. Jeff's company is JW2E, Inc., a Website development, design, and hosting company located in Channahon, Illinois.

Updates and Authentication Services

The Website, www.barclaytoys.com, contains updates to the tables of known varieties found in the book, updates to the text of the book, additional information that has been discovered, pictures of new varieties, and other information of interest to collectors of these toys. The Website also gives information concerning authentication services for these toys as well as email contact information for the authors. Although this book is based on the examination of well over 15,000 examples, many of the varieties and colors listed in the book are quite scarce and there are almost certainly additional variations that exist, but that are not yet listed. Since color pictures can often be misleading, the authors only include as "existing" those pieces that they have actually seen.

Editorial Conventions

When the name of a specific series of the Barclay Transports appears in the text, this reference is capitalized. This convention is also utilized in respect to colors. When the name of a specific Barclay color appears in the text, this reference is capitalized. When the name of a color is a generic reference, it is not capitalized.

Contents

Barclay's Auto Transports

These inexpensive toys brought endless hours of pleasure to four generations of children. Barclay's Auto Transports were introduced in 1932 or 1933 and were produced continuously for almost forty years. These small, imaginative, metal toys were meant for play. The toys were inexpensive, had great styling, and were colorfully painted. They had pivoting trailers, wheels that rolled, and were very sturdy. The Barclay Auto Transports also had a considerable degree of detail in their designs, particularly in the first

An array of Barclay Auto Transport sets. Clockwise: Modern 4-car set; Streamlined set; Classic 2-car set with cast trailer with rare Yellow coupe; Vintage set; and Classic 4-car set.

three series. The colors were varied; however, they were generally primary and bright. Colors such as Red, Orange, Blue, and Green remained throughout the production period. Other colors were added or dropped as the various series evolved and as tastes changed. As production moved into the late 1960s, the colors became more varied and even brighter.

The Barclay Manufacturing Company, Inc., closed its doors very abruptly in 1971. There is relatively little detailed information written about the Company and even less about the miniature transports and cars. Even in the face of little published information, the Barclay auto transport toys have become very popular with collectors. This book attempts to document everything that is known about these toys as well as provide a detailed catalog of the various series and variations.

About the Barclay Manufacturing Company

Our information concerning the Barclay Manufacturing Company comes from the various existing toy catalogs, particularly those originally authored by Richard O'Brien, and from conversations with a variety of toy industry veterans and collectors familiar with the Company. The Barclay Manufacturing Company of New Jersey was organized in either late 1923 or early 1924.[1] It was named after "Barclay" Street (now 10th Street) in West Hoboken, New Jersey, and as it grew, the Company moved to various locations in northern New Jersey, the last being 316 Palisade Avenue in Union City, New Jersey.[2]

Originally owned by Leon Donze, Michael Levy bought an interest in the company in the 1920s and took control of the company around 1932.[3] Until the 1940s, most of Barclay's product was manufactured by the traditional slush casting method. In this process, a combination of metals, the main ingredient being lead, was poured into bronze molds. The mold was then rocked back and forth and the metal that was still liquid was poured out to create a hollow casting. In the 1940s, the company began to switch to an injection die-cast casting method, whereby metal was forced under pressure into a hollow opening in the mold. Once the metal cooled and hardened, the mold was opened to remove the finished casting. Although Barclay created a wide variety of toys, most of their success was with military and later civilian toy figures as well as all types of vehicles, both military and civilian. The company prospered throughout the 1920s and 1930s and was said to be the country's largest producer of lead alloy vehicles during the 1930s and early 1940s.

Barclay ran its manufacturing operation at several different locations. In the late 1930s, it was located on 52nd Street in West New York, New Jersey. William Lango, a noted toy collector and author, recounts a discussion with an elderly gentleman who lived near the West New York factory:

> The Barclay factory had cantilevered windows and some of the local kids would stand on the sidewalk outside the fence, and shout at employees who could see through the open windows. At one time, the kids even tossed a few stones at the windows. Infuriated Barclay workers would get so angry that once a worker tossed both soldiers and vehicles at the neighborhood kids. The kids ran back, picked up the soldiers and vehicles off the sidewalk, and ran like hell.
>
> At the West New York Factory, Barclay stored damaged, unsaleable soldiers outside, along side the building in open topped 55-gallon drums. When the drums were filled up, they were wheeled back into the plant and their contents were remelted. Neighborhood kids would sometimes climb the fence and help themselves to figures and vehicles.

Barclay suspended toy production on April 1, 1942, and began manufacturing metal components for the United States military effort for the duration of World War II.[4] Toy production resumed in 1945 after the war ended. While Barclay achieved some success in the 1950s, it continued to produce the same types of toys that had been popular thirty years before and began a progressive decline. Michael Levy's son-in-law, Stanley Goldsmith, joined the company in 1961 and assumed control of Barclay upon Levy's death in 1964.[5] Although Goldsmith introduced innovations such as the blister packs, Barclay continued to struggle and closed abruptly in 1971. At this time, the factory was located in Union City, New Jersey.

It is not known what instigated Barclay's sudden closure. Residents of the area say that when Barclay closed, its owners simply walked away from the unsecured plant leaving molds, stocks of boxes, and much more. Local scrap and antique dealers later picked up many of the abandoned bronze molds. At least some of these molds eventually were sold to private collectors. In 1976, Lango located one of the bronze molds used to produce cars for the post-war transports. This mold was being used as a boat anchor in the Hudson River. Lango also reports that at the time the plant closed, a dumpster was parked in the street and was filled with all sorts of figures and castings. This dumpster and other dumpsters on the property were pilfered by neighborhood residents. Even several years after the Company closed, collectors visiting the shuttered plant found abandoned boxes, axles, and other components.

One possible explanation of the closure was the fact that lead in toys had first been identified as a serious health risk to children in the late 1960s. At this time, the Toy Manufacturers of America (TMA) and the American Academy of Pediatrics introduced drastic limitations on the use of lead and lead paint in toys. One might speculate that the cost of changing Barclay's production methods as well as the potential product and environmental liability arising from past production led to the decision that it was best just to shut down.

How This Book Was Compiled

This book represents knowledge accumulated over several decades of collecting by several major collectors, discussions with former employees of Barclay, store sale catalogs, and other sources. The project actually began as an attempt to put together a collection inventory. As with many types of toys made by defunct toy companies, very little has been documented concerning the Barclay Manufacturing Company in general and virtually nothing specifically concerning the Auto Transports. This situation is further complicated by an almost complete absence of catalogs and other contemporary materials.

One of the challenging aspects of many types of collecting is the scarcity of information. This is particularly true of items from a company such as Barclay Manufacturing, which produced a wide variety of inexpensive toys and then simply closed its doors. In contrast to the typical collectible toy catalog, this book provides detailed descriptions, drawings, and pictures including variations, paint colors, and identifiers. In addition to the authors' collections, the authors had access to several major collections of the Barclay Auto Transports as well as the knowledge of a number of collectors and former Barclay employees.

Classic 4-car trailer set with traditional colors and configuration of cars

The authors are the first to acknowledge that there is more to learn about the series. It is hoped that the collectors and readers of this book will contribute their recollections and knowledge to clarify and augment the information already gathered.

Collecting the Barclay Transports and Cars

Given the variety of trucks and cars in the various series, these toys can be collected in any number of ways. You can collect a few pieces that you like, collect a given series, collect the major varieties and/or colors, or collect all or part of one or more series by each detailed variety. You can collect sets, the cars alone, or collect both sets and the individual cars. Our detailed listings are intended for every interested collector's edification and in no way should be viewed as a recommendation as to how the various series should be collected.

As far as is known, the first two series were only sold as sets; although today you do see the pieces being sold individually. The trailers and cabs were sold as parts of sets that included the required number of cars throughout the production of the four series. At least by the early 1950s, the cars from the Third or Classic Series were being sold individually in five and dime stores for five cents apiece. From approximately 1961 through the final days of production, the individual cars were sold primarily in bubble packs containing seven cars to a pack. Detailed discussions of the packaging and distribution of the various series can be found later in the book under those titles.

Numbering, Varieties, and Nomenclature

As is the case with many collectible toys, numbering has been problematic and spotty. The numbering (beginning with the letters "BV") found in O'Brien's books is helpful; however, it only focuses on the basic sets, does not address the variations,[6] and is scheduled for revision in coming updates of these books. The only known official Barclay numbering is in relation to the numbers on packaged sets of cars or transport sets. While cross-references to both the O'Brien numbers as well as to the Barclay numbers are provided, the toys require a much more specific and comprehensive numbering system. The numbering system that is adopted first identifies the piece as being a cab (C), a two-car trailer (2T), a four-car trailer (4T), a sedan (S), or a coupe (CO). The second component of the number identifies the series. There are four major series distinguished by the distinctive designs of the major components. The Third Series ran approximately twenty-six years. The Fourth Series in part overlapped the Third Series and ran approximately twelve years. The series also have names. The First Series is also referred to as the Vintage Series, the Second Series as the Streamlined Series, the Third Series as the Classic Series, and the Fourth Series as the Modern Series. These descriptions will be used interchangeably throughout the book.

Since the First Series cab has no variations, the cab in the first series is simply identified as C1. The Classic and Modern Series, in contrast, include numerous variations for each of the components. The second number in the Third and Fourth Series represents a major variation. The third number in these series represents a less significant variation within a major variation; and in a few cases, a fourth number represents still another level of variation. As an example, a four-car trailer from the 1945-1964 era is numbered as 4T3.1.1, which identifies this piece as being a four-car trailer that is part of the Third Series. The second number after the piece identifier says the piece is the first major variation within this series of trailers and the third number identifies the piece as the first secondary variation of the first major variation of this trailer. With very few exceptions, every known variation that was part of the regular production, even when produced for a very short time, is included in the numbered variations. A few unusual variations are simply noted at the bottom of the identification grids or in the text and illustrations. These latter variations may or may not have been part of the regular production runs.

The decision to treat a particular variation as a major or a minor variation was based upon its apparent significance. As an example, the major variations in the sedans from the Classic Series represent the three distinctive variants in which this car appeared. Within the first variation of the sedan, called the "Plain Sedan," there are five sub-variations. The sub-variations are viewed as less significant compared to the three distinctive variations in the external appearance of these cars; therefore, cars within the sub-variations are identified as S3.1.1 through S3.1.5. While reproductions and alterations made outside the factory are discussed in a later section, they are not considered collectible and, therefore, are not identified in the numbering system.

Variations were created in several ways. First, the four series represent the four major designs. Second, from time to time changes were made in one or more pieces within a series such as the change from cast to aluminum trailers in the Third Series. Third, while maintaining the essential appearance of a piece, Barclay sometimes changed the molds, an example being when they went from open to closed wheel-wells in the Classic Series cars and cabs. Fourth, minor variations were created by changing components such as the various changes of wheels in the cars within the Modern Series. Fifth, as molds began to wear, there was evidently a tendency to rework the older molds. This fact appears to explain some of the variations in the cars of the Classic Series. Sixth, some varieties may have been created by various manufacturing practices. As an example, it is not clear whether the open and closed rear window varieties of the cars in the earlier part of the Fourth Series were the result of different molds or the result of some aspect of the manufacturing process that sometimes failed to punch out the back window.

We must remember that these were toys and very inexpensive toys at that. Consequently, there was an effort to never waste materials. Older parts, if they happened to be available, were used on a transitional basis such as the use of the white wheels on the aluminum trailers in the Third Series. A number of transitional variations were created because parts for older varieties were used as parts on newer varieties. This same factor applies to color variations. On occasion, Barclay used the paints and parts that were available. While there appears to have been set color schemes for the various sets, from time to time other paint colors were used. With the exception of some of the hot colors in the latter years of the Fourth Series, the new colors that appeared were typically colors that were being used on other Barclay products of the time, particularly the solders and other metal figures.

While we have cataloged all known variations, there are minor differences that we did not consider as legitimate variations. The most obvious example is minor paint shade and tint variations that arise in every series. In the case of every variation included, actual examples have been examined and authenticated as being produced in the Barclay factory.

The Major Series: A Brief Introduction

The most extensive part of this book is a very detailed description of the varieties within the four major series of Barclay Transports. At this point, we are only briefly describing each of the four series.

First or Vintage Series

Not a great deal is known about the Vintage Series. Other than color variations, there are no variations in the transport pieces and a single variation in the cars. It is believed that the First Series was manufactured between 1933 and the latter part of the 1930s. The cabs and the cars were made from a lead alloy and were manufactured by the traditional slush casting technique. This method resulted in castings that are somewhat thicker than the die-cast castings in the later series, which were produced by the injection die-cast casting method. Wheels on both the cabs and trailers were made of white natural rubber with red wooden hubs. The trailers were stamped from steel and painted. The cars exist in two varieties, sedans and coupes, and have metal wheels, a characteristic of all Barclay transport cars until 1965. There were no four-car transports in this series.

Second or Streamlined Series

As with the First Series, not a great deal is known about the Streamlined Series. It is believed that the series was manufactured from approximately 1938 through 1939. The cab has a more modern, "streamlined" look and is cast out of a lead alloy by the traditional slush casting method. A notable feature of the cab is the word "Trailer" cast into the door area on each side of the cab. The wheels on the cab are the same as those described for the First Series; however, the wheels typically do not have the wooden hubs.

The trailers are the same as the trailers in the First Series except they typically lack the wooden hubs. The cars are the same as and indistinguishable from the cars in the First Series. As with the First Series, there were no four-car transports in the Streamlined Series.

Classic 2-car trailer set with Orange cast trailer

Third or Classic Series

The Third Series is what most people think of when the Barclay Auto Transports are mentioned. This series is notable given its length of production, 1939 through 1965, and its variety of colors and other variations. It was also the first series to include both two and four-car transports. As with the First and Second Series, the cabs and the cars were cast out of a lead alloy and painted; however, in this case they were manufactured by the injection die-cast casting process. Before World War II, the two-car trailers were also cast out of a lead alloy and painted. After World War II, all trailers, both two-car and four-car, were made from metal, primarily unpainted aluminum with side supports for the four-car trailers made from steel. The cars in this series come in sedans and coupes with metal wheels and exist in a number of variations.

Fourth or Modern Series

The Fourth Series represented Barclay's attempt to modernize its line. The cabs were relatively detailed. While more modern in appearance, the cars lack most of the detail found in the earlier series. As with the Third Series, the cabs and cars were cast using the injection die-cast casting method, while the trailers were aluminum. The earliest cars retained the metal wheels; however, the later cars had rubber and then plastic wheels. The last type of cars in the series had a single piece plastic axle and wheel assembly. This final variety reflected the gradual deterioration of quality in the later years of Barclay's operation.

Identification and Description

Dating

Dating the various components and variations found in the Barclay Transport Series is somewhat problematic. Dating is complicated by the almost total non-existence of contemporary information from the Barclay Manufacturing Company itself. To the best of our knowledge, no contemporary resource exists concerning these toys and the catalogs that have been seen are fragmentary at best. The dates included are based upon the best existing information and are subject to change. The production dates of the series themselves are generally correct. The dates of certain variations can be deduced from other facts, an example being the white rubber tires used on the first two series and the earlier varieties of the third series. We know that white rubber ceased to be used on toys in the early part of the World War II era because rubber was needed for the war effort and was rationed. Another technique is to compare known mint sets. While the contents of most sets have been altered with various substitutions, there are examples of mint sets where the owner knows when a particular set was purchased or that it was purchased with all of its original wrappings. Additional knowledge has been gained from store catalogs, former employees, and advertisements.

One of the factors complicating dating for the Barclay Auto Transports was the Company's tendency to continue to use old parts, the periodic reworking of the molds, experimentation with new materials, and overlapping production of certain variations and/or series. Examples of the use of older parts and reworking the molds have already been mentioned. An example of experimentation with new materials is the existence of copper-coated steel trailers in the Third Series. The fact that the cars of the Third and Fourth Series were produced simultaneously for several years is an example of the overlapping of some series. For the most part, discrete dates are used, meaning that one series is dated as ending a given year and the next set is assumed to have been manufactured in the next year. In reality, a new series or variation could have been issued at any time of the year. It is also likely that multiple series and/or variations in fact were produced at the same time and, therefore, overlapped.

Condition

Throughout this catalog, the ten-point "C" scale frequently used in toy collecting catalogs and auctions has been adopted. On this scale, the collectible grades are roughly:

C6 Good: Played with condition with overall wear. While played with, all parts are present and all paint is original. Considered collectible by many collectors. Inside of cars and cabs may be discolored.

C7 Good Plus: Overall wear, but noticeably less wear than C6. All parts are present and all paint is original.

C8 Very Good: Minor overall wear, clean, very good color and overall condition. At least hints of luster on the inside of the casting and on the metal wheels of cars and cabs.

C9 Excellent: Near mint, minor chips and abrasions. The inside of the cars and cabs as well as the metal wheels should be bright and shiny. There should be little to no rust on the metal axles. The piece should be clean and the paint should be bright.

C10 Mint: Mint means exactly as the piece came from the factory. The piece may be self-standing, mint in a box (MIB), mint in a package (MIP), or mint on a card (MOC) in the case of the bubble packs. Each piece must be clean and bright. There must be original luster on the inside and wheels of cars and cabs. There should be no rust on the metal axles.

Judging conditions is complicated by several factors. Since the Barclay Auto Transports were inexpensive toys, they were not necessarily delivered from the factory in pristine, flawless condition. It is very common to see one or more pieces with minor chips and abrasions even though they have never been out of their original packaging. This is even true of cars in the seven-piece bubble pacts with absolutely no possibility of have rubbed against another piece. Pieces can also be found with manufacturing flaws, which are still absolutely mint.

Common flaws include fragments of metal on the casting, extra metal in the windows, thin spots in the metal, and small cracks or holes. Painting is another issue. While painting will be discussed later in detail, the quality of paint jobs varied greatly. The quality of the paint jobs depended upon when the piece was produced, the care or lack of care applied when the piece was painted, and the color of the paint. The most common painting flaw is incomplete coverage. Pieces can also be found with little or no wear from play but with rusted axles and discolored interiors and wheels. Rust is also frequently seen on the steel supports on the four-car transports. The rust on the axles is typically the result of moisture. Discoloration of the lead is the result of oxidation. Oxidation occurs naturally, however, it can be hastened if the piece is in a moist area for an extended period. Discoloration of the lead can also occur from the oils of the skin when it is handled with bare hands.

Rarity

Except in the case of the most knowledgeable collectors, rarity has not been widely acknowledged within the various series of Barclay Auto Transports. In truth, there is a tremendous range of rarity within the various series. We have used a rarity scale with ranges from R-1 (very common) to R-10 (unique):

R-1 Most Common

R-2 Common, But Less Often Seen Than R-1

R-3 Seen, But Relatively Infrequently

R-4 Scarce, Seen But Difficult to Locate

R-5 Very Scarce, Difficult to Locate

R-6 Extremely Scarce, Seldom Seen

R-7 Rare, Few Examples Known To Exist

R-8 Very Rare, 5 – 10 Examples Exist

R-9 Extremely Rare, 2 - 4 Examples Exist

R-10 Unique

It can be surmised that millions of pieces of the various Barclay Auto Transports were produced. Based upon observations at toy shows and auctions, however, it appears that most of these toys were destroyed and/or discarded many years ago. While both sets and individual pieces are seen, most examples are used. Of the pieces and sets offered for sale, one generally sees only the more common variations. Certain pieces, varieties, and colors are scarce to rare and some pieces are in the R-8 to R-10 categories. The listings attempt to give some feeling for the relative rarity of various pieces. There is no attempt to differentiate the rarity of pieces in various conditions; therefore, only one rarity number is assigned to each piece. This is meant to give an indication of the relative rarity of that piece across all conditions. It is clear that true C-9 and C-10 pieces are scarce in virtually all varieties and very rare in the more scarce varieties.

In general, we have assigned a rarity of no higher than R-7, although it is our belief that a number of the pieces listed are in the R-8 to R-10 categories. The rarity scales are based upon the actual observation of approximately 15,000 pieces, primarily cars. As more information surfaces and more people become aware of the variations and their relative scarcity, these initial assignments will necessarily have to be updated.

Pricing

Pricing the Barclay Auto Transports is difficult. While these items are actively sought after and rising in price, only the most knowledgeable buyers and sellers differentiated pricing between the relative common and the much more scarce varieties. The prices listed in this catalog are the prices a knowledgeable collector is willing to pay for an example in an arms-length transaction. Given the facts that many transactions occur without the rarity being fully articulated and that even mint specimens can vary in quality, prices are given in relatively large ranges.

Production and Painting

Production

First and Second Series

Very little is known regarding the production methods utilized to produce the First and Second Series. Clearly, the cabs and cars were produced in bronze molds into which a hot lead alloy was poured. We do not know how many pieces were produced simultaneously by each mold. In the first two series, the cabs and cars were first painted and then had the wheels attached by putting the axle through axle holes and crimping one end of the axle. Consequently, there should never be paint on the axles or tires. The trail-

Classic 4-car trailer set with Pink substituted for Red

ers were made from stamped steel and were painted after they had been shaped, but before the wheels were attached. The trailers for these two series are the same except that on the First Series the wheels included red wooden hubs, which are found on many Barclay vehicles of that era.

Third Series

Beginning in 1939, the cabs and the cars were manufactured from molds using the injection die-cast casting method. Although we do not know the number of pieces produced by each of the molds that produced the cabs, we do know that the molds casting the cars produced four castings at a time. In both cases, the molds were bronze into which hot metal was injected under pressure to produce the castings. While we do not know how many sets of molds were used, we do know that there were two distinct varieties of the early sedans and one variety of the early coupes. Each of the three different early cars as well as the early cabs had open wheel-wells.

At various times the molds were reworked. A major change occurred in the late 1940s or early 1950s, when the wheel-wells were closed. Subsequent reworking of the molds or the creation of new molds produced the Grill Bars Sedan. Reworking and gradual deterioration of one or more molds appears to have eventually produced the Crooked-Line Coupe and the No-Line Coupe. With these three additional varieties, there are three major varieties for each of the Third Series sedans and the Third Series coupes. About 1954 new molds were again created to produce four-cars at a time. In this case, all were Plain Sedans and coupes with closed wheel-wells. These molds were used until production of the Third Series stopped in approximately 1965.

With the exception of some early examples produced just as the Third Series began, castings were painted after the casting was produced and before the wheels were attached. The final step in the production process was to attach the axles and wheels as had been done for the first two series.

Initially, the trailers for the Classic Series were cast, painted, and then had the axles and wheels attached. When production resumed after World War II, Barclay began using stamped, unpainted metal trailers. These stamped trailers were manufactured for Barclay by

Heyco Products, Inc., which was located in Kenilworth, N.J. In most cases, the principal components were stamped from aluminum, while the pieces connecting the ramps on the four-car trailers were stamped from steel. A tab to hold the cars on the lower ramp on the four-car trailers was stamped from either aluminum or steel. After creating the various pieces, the components of the four-car trailers were connected by means of rivets and then the axles and wheels were added. As with the cabs and cars, the axles on the trailers had a nub at one end and were crimped at the other.

Fourth Series

Production of these cars began about 1957 and production of the cabs began about 1965. The Fourth Series cabs and cars were produced by the injection die-cast casting method. The cars were produced from molds producing either multiple sedans or multiple coupes. While each car was numbered 1-8 on the inside roof, we do not know the significance of the number. It is speculated that this number either refers to a specific mold or refers to the number of the casting within a single mold. After the hot metal was injected into the bronze molds to produce the castings, the castings were painted, and the axles and wheels were attached. There are a number of variations within the cars, which are also called "Shoebox" cars due to their shape. With minor variations, the trailers were the same as the trailers in the Third Series.

Colors

Color is one of the most intriguing and appealing aspects of the Barclay Auto Transports. Colors such as Red continued throughout the series. Other colors were added, while existing colors were dropped. While most colors were used for a period of years, other colors such as Gray, Moss, and Clay appear to have been used for only a matter of days or weeks. These were inexpensive toys and care was not always taken to keep colors consistent from one batch to the next. Consequently, colors such as the greens, oranges, and blues come in a variety of shades and tints.

In the First and Second Series, we see a limited pallet of bright, primary colors: Green, Orange, Blue, Red, and Yellow. The initial years of the Third Series included relatively few colors. In addition to the five colors in the First and Second Series, multiple shades of Green and Blue appeared in the first ten to fifteen years of the series. From the mid-1950s until the end of the series in the 1960s, several other colors appeared including Brown, Camel, Clay, Cream, Flesh, Gray, Magenta, Pink, Salmon, Tan, and Lemon Yellow. In contrast to the earlier practice of continuing colors for a very long time, many of these colors appeared in the transitional period when cars from both the Third and Fourth Series were produced simultaneously. In some cases, colors appear to have been used for no more than a few weeks. While some colors were used on various combinations of cabs and cars, other colors only appear on one or another type of car. In the detailed discussion of each series, the relative rarity of the various colors will be addressed as they relate to specific pieces within the various series. The colors in the Third Series that were introduced in the transitional period are among the most scarce in any series.

Colors in the beginning of the Fourth Series largely duplicated the colors used in the last part of the Third Series; however, the last version of this series includes a substantial expansion of colors including extensive use of "bright" or "hot" colors. The hot colors were achieved by using a white base paint and then spraying automobile paint over the base to give the piece a bright eye-catching color, some of which are very difficult to locate.

The criteria for including a specific color is that it be readily identifiable as a distinct color, that there was consistency in its use, that it is clearly a product of the factory, and that it is not simply a shade or tint variation. Colors are discussed and illustrated extensively in the Detailed Catalog. Shading and tint differences are particularly pronounced in the Third Series. Differences occurred both over different periods of time, i.e. the Forest Green in the earlier years of the Classic Series differs from the Forest Green in the later years of the Classic Series; and within the same period of time when sequential batches of paint were mixed with slight differences.

We also know that non-standard paint combinations were sometimes produced in the factory. According to William Lango, two older female ex-employees related how some of the young women in the finishing department would flirt with the men in the paint department to get them to paint figures in special colors. To prove the point they produced examples of metal sailors painted pink instead of the traditional white.

Painting

The transport cabs and cars were cast in groups. Once the castings were removed from the molds, the group was lined up and painted in mass before the axles and wheels were added. Since the pieces were spray painted, you can expect some paint on the inside of the pieces with open windows. With rare exceptions, pieces were never painted on the inside and never repainted with another color. Evidence of paint of another color on the inside of the piece, a complete coat of paint on the inside, paint on a wheel, or paint on an axle is generally an indication that the piece has been painted outside the factory.

There are a very few examples of genuine cars and cabs, which were painted one color and then were returned to the paint line and repainted a second color. If a casting turned over during the painting process and failed to receive a complete coat of paint, on occasion such pieces were put aside and later repainted. If the color of the paint line changed before the piece was repainted, this resulted in a repainted example. There is at least one example of a cab that had already been repainted and then was again returned to the line and repainted with a third color. In these cases, there will be splashes of all the colors of paint in the inside of the pieces having open windows. There are also examples of early Classic Series cars, which were completely painted on the inside as well as early Classic Series and Modern Series cars that were painted after the wheels were attached. These variations will be discussed and illustrated in the Detailed Catalog.

Distribution and Packaging

Distribution

Barclay toys were primarily sold in five and dime stores. They were commonly found at stores such as Woolworth's, Kresges, TG&Y, and many others as well as at value department stores such as The Fair in Chicago. For many years, Woolworth's was Barclay's largest customer. This channel of distribution also contributed to our limited knowledge concerning these toys. In contrast to more upscale retailers that produced extensive catalogs, most of the major outlets selling Barclay toys issued no more than an occasional sale flyer compounding the difficulty of locating contemporary information concerning these toys.

Packaging

Early Packaging

As far as is known, the First, Second, and the earlier part of the Third Series were only sold in two-car trailer sets. The earliest packaging known is for the very early sets from the Third Series, which consisted of flat pieces of cardboard with slits to hold the wheels. Each piece had its own position with the cars having positions off the trailer. Since Barclay used this method of packaging for its military and civilian figures in the 1930s, it is certainly possible that the earlier sets from the First and Second series were packaged in a similar fashion.

Two mint Classic 4-car sets in cardboard boxes

Cardboard Boxes

The first known box packaging was for the four-car transport sets. The packaging is printed red, white, and blue on cardboard. On the back is a drawing of a transport unloading its cars. One piece that is often missing from the boxed sets is a flat piece of loose cardboard that fits in the bottom of the box. This piece served as an anchor for two rubber bands that were wrapped around the transport set to hold the set in place. When these rubber bands are present, they are deteriorated. Although it is not precisely known when this packaging first appeared, it is very likely that it began to be used when the four-car trailer set was first introduced shortly after the end of World War II. This packaging continued until the switch to the bubble packages sometime after 1957. Given Barclay's tendency to produce product in parallel, it is quite possible that the cardboard box continued to be used at the same time that other product was being sold in the bubble packs. Barclay did not mark these boxes with prices, although individual stores often did so. This packaging always contains a Third Series cab, a four-car trailer, two sedans, and two coupes.

As you look at the box, the typical early Classic Series' configuration within the package is for the cab to be facing right with an Orange sedan on the upper left, a Green sedan on the upper right, a Red coupe on the lower left, and a Blue coupe on the lower right. As time evolved, other configurations can be found, frequently with straight substitutions, such as Pink or Salmon being substituted for Red, Camel or Yellow being substituted for Orange, and Forest Green being substituted for Light Green. Third Series colors such as Cream, Hot Pink, and Silver, do not appear to have been included in the trailer sets. These latter colors are thought to have only been found in the circle packs that began to be sold in the early 1960s.

The cars in the boxed sets are normally the Third Series cars; however, there are also cardboard boxes that contain a mixture of cars from the Third and Fourth Series. Normally the cab and trailer have black wheels. There is at least one example of a mint white wheeled set in this packaging; however, it is not clear that this is the original configuration. While one could question whether the Shoebox cars were originally in these sets, the number of mint sets containing one or more Shoebox cars clearly suggests that this packaging continued until sometime after the introduction of the Shoebox cars.

Boxes of the four-car sets were wrapped in newspaper and shipped in cardboard boxes containing various quantities. With the exception of the flat cardboard packaging for the early two-car sets, there does not appear to have been any special packaging for either individual cars or the two-car transport sets before the introduction of the bubble pack.

Bubble Packs

Sometime in the late 1950s, the bubble pack packaging was introduced. There were three types of sets. The #330 for the two-car transport set, the #440 for the four-car transport set, and the #339 for a mixture of seven individual sedans and coupes in different colors. The typical color configuration for the cars in the #339 package was two Red cars and one car each of Green, Blue, and Orange, plus cars in two other colors such as Beige, Yellow, Pink, or Silver. Later bubble packs contained a more varied combination of cars. There were at least five distinct types of bubble packs used, each of which is listed in the sequence below:

Yellow base with black printing: This type of bubble pack exists in all three set variations. The cab is always the Third Series cab. The most common cars are the Third Series cars; however, it is not unusual to see mixtures of the Third and the Fourth Series cars in these sets. The #330 set has a printed price of 29 cents, the #440 set has a printed price of 59 cents, and the #339 set has a printed price of 49 cents.

Yellow base and Metal Mites bubble packs

White base with red and blue printing: This bubble pack has been seen in the #440 version, and the #330 version. The #330 version has a printed price of 49 cents. The cab is always the Third Series cab.

Yellow base on white background with red printing: This bubble pack variation is seen in all three sets. The cab is always the Third Series cab; however, the cars are a mixture of the Third and the Fourth Series cars. The #330 set has a printed price of 29 cents, the #440 set has a printed price of 59 cents, and the #339 set has a printed price of 49 cents.

Metal Mites and yellow base on white background bubble packs

White base with red and blue graphics and writing: This is the "Metal Mites" type of bubble pack. The set consists of Fourth Series cabs and cars. The #330 set has a printed price of either 39 or 49 cents, the #440 set has a printed price of 59 cents, and the #339 set has a printed price of 69 cents. At least one example of the #440 set exists with the price circle blacked out by hand before the plastic bubble was attached to the cardboard.

Blue, black, and purple base printed on white with black and purple lettering printed on yellow: This is the last variation of the bubble pack. The set consists of the Fourth Series cabs and cars in a #440 set.

Barclay produced special packaging for several of its larger customers and a number of additional varieties of bubble pack packaging do exist.

Reproductions and Out-of-the-Factory Alterations

Since we do not consider reproductions and out-of-the-factory alterations collectible, we do not dwell on these pieces. At a minimum, reproductions have been made of the Third Series trailers, both aluminum and cast, and the Third Series cars. These reproductions can generally be spotted due to variations in the thickness of the metal, the cutting techniques used for the trailers, the type of axles and tires, the thickness and quality of the castings, the paint colors, the method of painting, and other details.

The principal alteration encountered is painting done outside of the factory. Examples include colors that do not match, colors that never existed, two-tone combinations, and painting by brush. Aside from the use of non-standard colors, it is almost impossible to paint the Barclay pieces with the wheels on and it is almost impossible to take the wheels off and then duplicate the construction of the axle. Even when the color and painting technique is matched, pieces painted outside the factory generally contain traces of the original color on the underside as well as paint on the wheels.

Authentication

It is assumed that additional varieties may exist within the various series discussed. This is particularly the case in respect to the existence of additional colors of some of the varieties in the Modern Series. Information concerning authentication of Barclay Transport toys, whether new varieties or existing varieties, can be found at www.barclaytoys.com.

Detailed Catalog: First or Vintage Series

The First or Vintage Series is seldom seen. Since none of the pieces has any indication of the manufacturer, many collectors of the later series do not realize that the transports and cars from the First and Second Series are related to the transports and cars of the later series. The only significant variations are in color and in the cars, which are found with both open and closed windows. The series was manufactured between 1932 or 1933 and the late 1930s. Hot metal was poured into brass molds to produce the castings for the cabs and cars. Paint was applied to the casting by spraying. Axles were inserted and the wheels were added after the paint was dry.

Original Vintage trailer sets

Vintage Series Colors

The colors used in the Vintage Series are relatively straightforward. There are four distinct colors, Green, Orange, Red, and Yellow. As with virtually all of the Barclay colors, various shading and tint differences exist. The darker Green was used relatively consistently on the cabs and cars with a lighter shade used on the steel trailers. The shading and tint of Red is relatively consistent, but there are slight variations. Orange was only used on the cars; however, there are significant shade and tint differences ranging from a very light shade to a dark shade similar to the Burnt Orange in the Modern Series. Yellow was only used on the cars. This shade of Yellow is the same bright shade seen on the early cars in the Classic Series.

Scarcity and pricing is listed in italics after the detailed description for each piece. Due to variations seen in the market, prices are listed in ranges for examples in C-8 (Very Good) and C-10 (Mint) conditions.

First or Vintage Series (Cabs, Trailers, Sedans, and Coupes)				Green	Orange	Red	Yellow
C1	(BV152)	1932-37	Cast, White Wheels, Red Hubs, Model A Ford	■		■	
2T1	(BV152)	1932-37	Steel, White Wheels, Red Hubs, Painted	■		■	
S1	(BV152 or 114)	1932-38	Cast, Metal Wheels, Closed Windows		■		■
S2	(BV152 or 114)	1932-38	Cast, Metal Wheels, Open Windows		■		
CO1	(BV152 or 114)	1932-38	Cast, Metal Wheels, Closed Windows	■		■	
CO2	(BV152 or 114)	1932-38	Cast, Metal Wheels, Open Windows			■	

Vintage Series Cabs

The cabs are two and one-quarter inches long and have an open window on each side. As is the case with all the cast pieces in the various series, the cabs were spray painted on the outside; however, the inside should be the original silver color just as it came out

Vintage cabs, Green and Red. Note red wooden hubs

of the mold except where paint may have come through the windows. The cabs have a rectangular shape, look as if they belong to the 1920s or early 1930s, and appear to be modeled after the Model A Ford trucks of this era. A distinguishing characteristic of the cabs and trailers is the addition of a red, wooden hub on each wheel similar to the hubs on many Barclay vehicles of this era. On both the cabs and trailers, the wheels were made of natural, white rubber. Green is the most common color for the cabs. The Red cabs are the scarcer variety.

R-4: Green ($10-15) ($30-60)
R-5: Red ($20-25) ($40-70)

Vintage Series Trailers

In contrast to the later trailers, the trailers in the First Series are made from stamped metal with paint on both sides of the trailer platform. The trailers are three and one-quarter inches long. The underside is painted a light blue, whereas, the upper part of the trailer is either Light Green or Red. As with the cabs, the Green trailers are the most common and Red is somewhat scarcer. The wheels are white rubber with a red hub on each wheel.

R-4: Light Green, Red ($15-20) ($30-60)

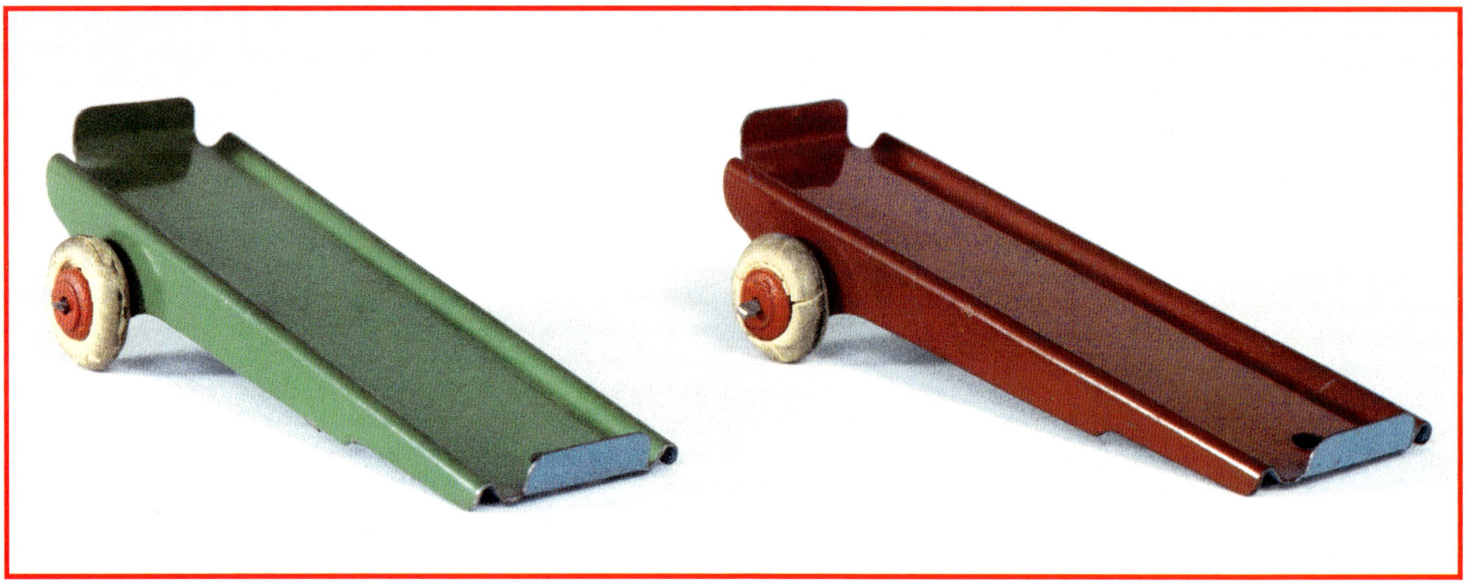

Vintage trailers, Green and Red. Note red wooden hubs

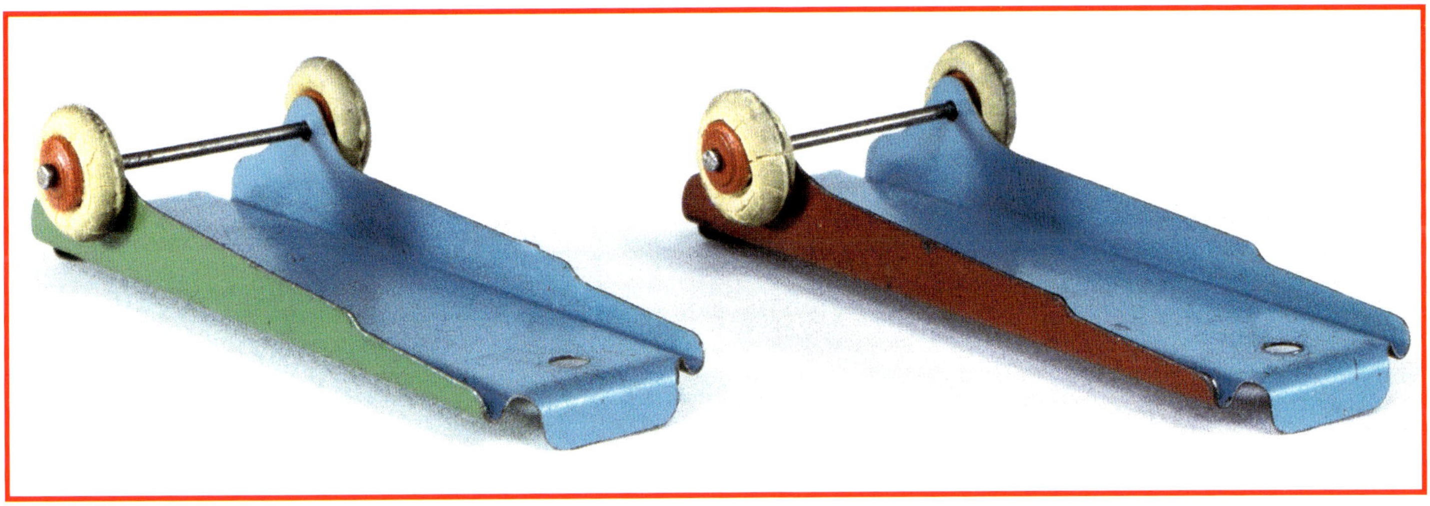

Vintage trailers, painted undersides

Vintage Series Cars

As is the case throughout the various series, the cars come in two varieties, sedans and coupes. All of the cars have metal wheels, a characteristic of all Barclay Transport cars until 1965. The sedan is one and one-half inches long, whereas the coupe is one and five-eights inches long. Unlike the later cars, most examples of these cars do not have open windows. The sedans are seen in various shades of Orange, ranging from a very light shade to almost a burnt orange shade, and Yellow. The coupe is found in Red, with minor shade and tint variations, and Green. The Orange sedans and the Red coupes are by far the most common. These cars should not be confused with similar Barclay vehicles that measure two inches long.

Vintage Transport cars, Orange sedan, Green coupe, and Red coupe, all with closed windows

Sedans Closed Windows
R-3: Orange ($10-15) ($20-30)
R-7: Yellow ($50-70) ($90-110)

Sedans Open Windows
R-6: All Colors ($25-85) ($40-135)

Coupes Closed Windows
R-3: Red ($10-15) ($20-30)
R-5: Green ($15-20) ($30-50)

Coupes Open Windows
R-6: All Colors ($25-85) ($40-135)

Vintage Transport car, Orange sedan with open windows

Vintage Series Original Sets

Original sets are made up of pieces of similar age and condition. A matched original set is more difficult to locate than a set that combines pieces from multiple sources, which may vary in age and condition. A set consists of a cab, trailer, sedan, and coupe. Pricing is for a set with the most common pieces.

R-5: Matched Set ($80-100) ($140-200)

Vintage Series: Other Characteristics, Packaging, and Availability

Axles on all of the pieces are made from a pin with a nub on one end that is crimped on the other end; however, in the earlier cars, there are some examples of axles that were made from nails. Over time, the white natural rubber on the cabs and trailers tends to turn color, becoming dry and brittle. All of the tires on an original set should show a similar degree of aging. The older white tires tend to accumulate dirt. Even when an older tire is washed, the tire will still appear to be off-white rather than the bright white of a new tire. If you find a white, new looking tire on these pieces, it is most certainly a replacement.

Recognizing mint or near mint specimens is somewhat challenging. Aside from a lack of chips, abrasions, and rust, the cast pieces in this series should be bright and shiny in the inside except where paint might have entered through open windows. Some pieces may appear to be mint, but have a darkened inside. This is the result of natural oxidation, which may have been compounded by the presence of moisture. As noted, white rubber tires age naturally. Even on mint specimens, they will appear off-white and may have cracks. This is a natural part of the aging process for this material and does not necessarily indicate use. In contrast to the later series, there were no four-car transports in the First Series.

As far as is known, this series was sold in sets with a matching cab and trailer with two cars, one sedan and one coupe, in various colors. The most common color combination is a Green cab and trailer with an Orange sedan and a Red coupe. It is not known how these sets came packaged. It is known that the sets in the earliest part of the Third Series were displayed in the stores on flat pieces of cardboard with slits cut for the wheels. The First Series may have been displayed in a similar fashion or they may have been simply shipped in bulk and laid out individually for sale.

All pieces in this series are scarce. Mint or near mint pieces are extremely scarce.

Detailed Catalog: Second or Streamlined Series

Not a great deal is known about the Second Series. The Second Series was most likely manufactured in 1938 and 1939. As with the First Series, there is no indication on any piece identifying the manufacturer; therefore, the various pieces are often incorrectly identified. Except for color, there are no variations in either the cabs or trailers. The cars are the same as in the First Series. As with the First Series, the cabs and cars were cast by pouring hot metal into brass molds using the traditional casting method. The trailers were stamped from steel. After each piece was painted, axles were inserted and the wheels were attached.

Original Streamlined trailer sets. From left to right: Blue, Green, and Red trailers with scarce Green coupe

Streamlined Series Colors

The colors used in the Streamlined Series are straightforward. Only three colors were used for the cabs and trailers. These are Blue, Red, and Green. In this case, the Green is lighter than that used in the First Series and the Blue is a Light Blue. The colors are relatively consistent and tend not to have the extreme shading and tint differences found in the later series.

Scarcity and pricing is listed in italics after the detailed description for each piece. Due to variations seen in the market, prices are listed in ranges for examples in C-8 (Very Good) and C-10 (Mint) conditions.

Second or Streamlined Series (Cabs and Trailers)				**Blue**	**Green**	**Red**
C2	(BV114)	1938	Cast, White Wheels, No Hubs, "Trailer" on Side			
2T2	(BV114)	1938	Steel, White Wheels, No Hubs, Painted			
Related Variety-Cab-C2 in Red with Built-up Hitch, Not Considered as Part of this Series						
Additional Variety-Cab and Trailer with Red Hubs						

Streamlined Series Cabs

The cabs are two and one-half inches long with windows on each side. The cab is clearly a more modern, streamlined design. The streamlined design was a characteristic of many manufactured products in the latter part of the 1930s. The cab was cast out of lead alloy by the traditional casting method. A notable feature of this cab is the word "Trailer" cast into the door area on each side.

Streamlined cab

As with the First Series, the inside of a mint cab should be the original silver color just as it came out of the mold except where paint may have come through the windows. The wheels on the cab are the same white, natural rubber as described for the First Series. The wheels typically do not have the red wooden hubs; however, examples of the cab with the red wooden hubs do exist. It is assumed that this latter variety was made during the transitional period as production moved from the First Series to the Second Series. The cab is only seen in Green.

R-4: Green ($15-20) ($30-60)

There are examples of a Red Streamlined Series cab with Black or White wheels and a built up hitch. Since this cab does not fit the Streamlined Series trailers or the later Classic Series trailers, it is assumed that it was intended for another Barclay toy. This cab variety is pictured for reference.

Streamlined cab with built-up back, not part of the Transport Toys

Streamlined Series Trailers

The trailers are stamped steel from the same die as the trailers in the First Series; however, they may or may not be painted on the under side. The trailers are three and one-quarter inches long. One notable difference between the trailers in the First Series and the Second Series is that the newer trailers typically do not have the wooden hubs on the wheels. Since a small number of Streamlined Series cabs exist with the red wooden hubs, it is assumed, however, that these cabs were sold with the older style trailer from the First Series that had wooden hubs. The white, natural rubber wheels are attached directly to the axles. The trailers are normally found in either Green or Red. Both colors are seen attached to Green cabs. The Blue trailers are a light shade in contrast to the darker shade frequently seen on the cast trailers in the early days of the Third Series. Blue trailers are extremely scarce.

R-4: Green, Red ($20-25) ($40-70)
R-6: Blue ($60-80) ($120-180)

Streamlined trailers, Green, Blue, and Red. Note lack of wooden hubs

Streamlined Series Cars

In all respects, the cars are the same as the cars in the First Series. Please refer to the First Series for discussion and pricing.

Streamlined Series Original Sets

Original sets are made up of pieces of similar age and condition. A matched original set is more difficult to locate than a set that combines pieces from multiple sources, which may vary in condition. A set consists of a cab, trailer, sedan, and coupe. Pricing is for a set with the most common pieces.

R-5: Matched Set ($80-100) ($140-200)

Streamlined Series: Other Characteristics, Packaging, and Availability

As with the First Series, axles on the cabs, trailers, and cars are made from a pin with a nub at one end that is crimped on the other end. Over time, the white natural rubber on the cabs and trailers tends to turn and become dry and brittle. On an original set, all of the tires should show a similar degree of aging and/or wear. If a tire is white and looks new, it is most likely a replacement tire.

Aside from lacking chips, abrasions, and rust, mint specimens of the cast pieces should be bright and shiny in the inside except where paint has entered through any open windows. Some pieces may have a darkened inside due to oxidation and excessive humidity. Even on mint specimens, the white rubber tires age naturally, will appear to be off-white, and may have cracks.

As far as is known, this series was only sold in sets of a cab, trailer, sedan, and coupe. It is not known whether the Second Series had packaging or not. Since it is known that early sets in the Third Series came on pieces of cardboard with slits cut for the various pieces, it is certainly possible that this series was sold in a similar fashion. Unlike the First Series, however, the Second Series was sold with contrasting colors for the cab and trailer as well as with the cab and trailer in the same color. The trailer set combinations are a Green cab with a Red, Green, or Blue trailer. In each case, the set came with two cars, most commonly a Red coupe and an Orange sedan. There were no four-car transports in the Second Series.

All pieces in this series are scarce. Mint or near mint pieces are very difficult to locate. Of the four components in the sets and for reasons that are unclear, the trailers seem to be the component that is the most difficult to find.

Detailed Catalog: Third or Classic Series

When the Barclay auto transport toys are mentioned, most collectors think of the Third or Classic Series for several reasons. First, it is the most common of the four series. Second, this series includes both two-car and the four-car transport sets. Third, the Third Series was sold in sets of the cab, transport, and matching cars; in sets of cars only; and the cars were sold individually. Fourth, there is a tremendous amount of variety in the series in terms of the castings, materials, and colors. The series was introduced in 1939 and continued until approximately 1965. While each piece in the new series was cast and the wheels were similar to the wheels in the Second Series, all of the pieces had a new design and used the injection die-cast casting process, which produced a thinner, more refined casting.

The cab and the cars in the Third Series appear to be from the late 1930s and many collectors find this series the most aesthetically appealing of the four series of this toy. The early cabs and

Original Classic trailer sets, Orange, Blue, and Yellow cast trailers

trailers in this series were marked with the "Barclay" name; however, the later cabs and trailers as well as all of the cars have neither the manufacturer nor the country of origin identified and are frequently misattributed to other manufacturers. A large number of varieties exist in each of the various pieces. In this section, we will systematically discuss and illustrate each of the known varieties and colors.

Classic Series Colors

In the earlier years of the Classic Series, seven colors were used; Light Blue, Blue, Forest Green, Light Green, Orange, Red, and Yellow. With the introduction of the closed wheel-well versions of the cars, the colors Camel, Pink, and Silver appeared. Moss Green and Gray are believed to have been produced in the 1957 to 1960 era; however, they apparently were manufactured for relatively short periods and were sold as part of the trailer sets. In the final years of production, the colors Brown, Chocolate, Clay, Cream, Flesh, Magenta, Salmon, Tan, and Lemon Yellow appeared. Of these transitional colors, Salmon, and Lemon Yellow were sold both in the

Original Classic 2-car and 4-car trailer sets with aluminum trailers

seven car circle packs as well as part of the trailer sets. Cream and Tan were definitely sold in the circle packs and may or may not have been sold as part of the trailer sets. It is not known when the colors Brown, Chocolate, Clay, Flesh, and Magenta were manufactured; however, it is safe to assume that they were also manufactured at the very end of the Classic Series production. Production of the Classic Series cars ceased about 1965.

In many of the colors, there are considerable differences in shading and tint. Shades can differ both between the same color produced in the earlier and later years of the Classic Series as well as between colors produced in sequential batches.

Known Shading and Tint Differences

Blue. A darker blue ranging from a very pure blue to almost a navy blue

Light Blue. Shades from light to somewhat darker

Brown. Based on one known example, the shade is a somewhat darker brown

Camel. Many shades going from lighter to darker-the color always has a yellowish orange tint

Chocolate. Based on one known example, a dark chocolate brown

Clay. At least two shade variations with one slightly lighter than the other-Clay has definite brown tint in contrast to the various shades found in the Orange range

Cream. Relatively consistent light off-white shade

Flesh. Based on one known example, a light brown used to color the flesh on Barclay's figurines

Gray. Varies from lighter to darker with one version of the lighter color appearing to have a pink tint

Forest Green. Earlier version has a blue tint; later version is close to an emerald green

Light Green. This common color varies from a relatively consistent lighter green to a somewhat darker version toward the end of the series

Moss Green. Relatively consistent with some shading and tint variation, a grayish green

Magenta. Consistent shading in the very few examples known, a bright pinkish color with a blue tint (this color is not illustrated)

Classic colors: Light Blue, Blue, Brown, Camel, and Cream

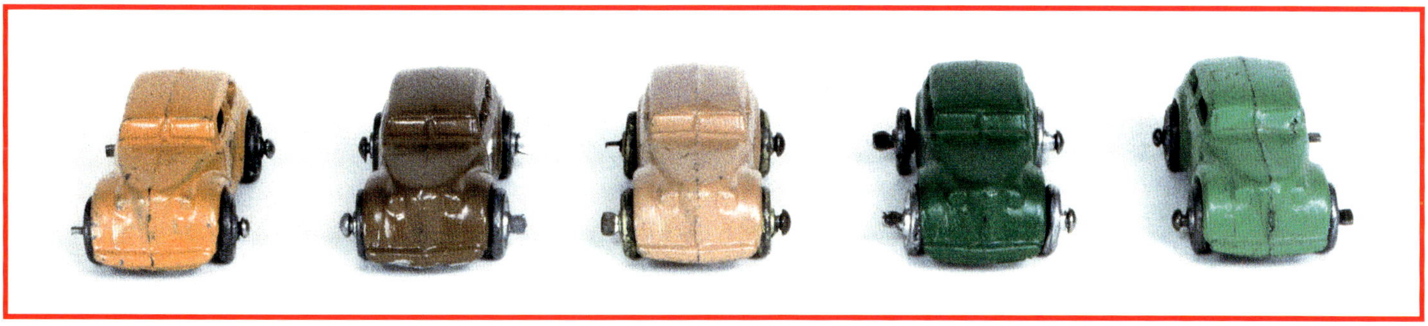

Classic colors: Clay, Chocolate, Flesh, Forest Green, and Light Green

Classic colors: Moss Green, Gray, Orange, Pink, and Red

Classic colors: Silver, Salmon, Tan, Yellow, and Lemon Yellow

Orange. Common color with relative consistency, however, in the later years of the series some examples tend to be darker, more of a tangerine

Pink. Color has considerable range with some examples appearing to be a washed out, light pink and others considerably brighter

Red. A common color used throughout the Classic Series that is fairly consistent, but can vary from a dark or burnt red to a very bright cherry red-differences are easiest seen on the cabs

Salmon. A relatively consistent color with minor shading differences; a reddish pink color

Silver. Probably the most consistent color in the series

Tan. Introduced in the later years of the series with minor variations in shading

Yellow. Almost a chrome yellow with minor variations of color

Lemon Yellow. Introduced in the final years of the series with minor variations in shading; yellow with a white tint

Scarcity and pricing is listed in italics after the detailed description for each piece. Due to variations seen in the market, prices are listed in ranges for examples in C-8 (Very Good) and C-10 (Mint) conditions.

Third or Classic Series Cabs				Blue	Blue-Lt.	Green-Lt.	Green-Moss	Gray	Orange	Pink-Lt	Red	Salmon
C3.1.1	(BV11)	1939-42	Cast, White Tires, Open Wheel-Wells, Low Hitch, '38 Ford Cab Over Engine			■					■	
C3.1.2	(BV11)	1939-40	Same as C3.1.1, Except Lights and Grill Mask Painted Silver								■	
C3.1.3	(BV75 or 157)	1945-46	Same as C3.1.1, Except Black Tires								■	
C3.2.1	(BV75 or 157)	1945-49	Cast, Black Wheels, Open Wheel-Wells, High Hitch, '38 Ford Cab Over Engine								■	
C3.2.2	(BV75 or 157)	1945-46	Same as C3.2.1, Except White Tires								■	
C3.3	(BV75 or 157)	1950	Cast, Black Wheels, Half Open Wheel-Wells, High Hitch, '38 Ford Cab Over Engine			■					■	
C3.4.1	(BV75 or 157) (330 or 440)	1950-65	Cast, Black Wheels, Closed Wheel-Wells, High Hitch, '38 Ford Cab Over Engine, Smooth Wheels	■	■	■		■	■	■	■	
C3.4.2	(BV75 or 157) (330 or 440)	1965	Same as C3.4.1, Except Ridged Wheels				■	■			■	■
C3.4.3	(BV75 or 157) (330 or 440)	1950-65	Same as C3.4.1, Except White Rubber Wheels								■	

Classic Series Cabs

The Third or Classic Series cab is approximately two and one-half inches long with four open windows, one on each of the two sides and two in front. The cab is thought to have been modeled after the 1938 Ford "cab over engine" truck cab. The earlier versions of this cab are the only cabs in the transport series to have the manufacturer identified. As with the earlier two series, the Third Series cab is cast, however, this time the casting is made with the die cast injection casting method. If the specimen is in mint condition, the inside of the cab should be shiny and silver in color with a small amount of paint having come through the windows.

With the possible exception of certain of the Third Series cars, the Third Series cab is probably the easiest piece to locate within the various series of Barclay Auto Transports. As with other pieces in the series, the metal axles are often seen with rust. Some exceptionally well-preserved pieces are still dull on the inside due to oxidation. The paint on the Classic Series pieces seems to have generally been well applied with full coverage and a reasonable resistance to the rigors of use. In contrast to the first two series, the cabs within the Third Series include several variations, which will be explained and illustrated below. Please remember that the dating is based on a combination of memory and deduction. These cabs pulled both the two-car and the four-car trailers. Virtually no records from the Barclay Manufacturing Company exist, and the exact dates of some of the variations may never be known.

Classic cabs: C3.1.3 and C3.1.1, low hitch and open wheel-wells. Note different tire colors.

Classic cab: C3.1.3, underside showing open wheel-wells

C3.1.1 The Third Series was introduced in 1939 and produced continually until Barclay ceased toy production in April 1942 to manufacture metal components for the World War II war effort. While the design was completely new, the cab had many of the same characteristics of the earlier cabs including white, smooth, natural rubber wheels. Two characteristics that are often overlooked are open wheel-wells and a low hitch. As will be discussed, the later specimens of this cab design have half and then fully closed wheel-wells. While the open wheel-well design continued for a short time after production was resumed in 1945, the molds were apparently modified within this timeframe and the hitch was raised. The adjustment of the hitch apparently was made to eliminate the tendency of the trailer to scrape the back portion of the cab when the trailer was connected to the low hitch.

While it is possible that a small number of this variation of the cab were produced after the World War II, it is generally assumed that most of the cabs with white rubber wheels were produced before the 1942 shutdown. Natural rubber was in short supply early in the war and was gradually replaced by synthetic rubber soon after the war began. This is the most common version of the early Third Series cabs, but it is still difficult to find in a true mint state with no paint loss, shiny interior, and no rust on the axles. This variety comes in two colors, Red and Light Green. The most common color is the Light Green. On the inside, you will find the words, "Barclay" and "Made in U.S.A.," identifying both the manufacturer and the country of origin. These identifiers are seen in all of the open wheel-well variations of this cab.

R-3: Light Green ($5-10) ($15-20)
R-4: Red ($10-15) ($20-30)

C3.1.2 As the Third Series was introduced, a number of experiments appear to have taken place with the new transports. This cab is the same as the C3.1.1 cab; however, both the lights and the grill have been painted silver by the mask painting method. This treatment is seen on a number of other Barclay vehicles in the 1930s. This variation is believed to have appeared in 1939 or 1940 soon after the Third Series was introduced, is only known to exist in Red, and is extremely scarce.

R-7: Red ($70-80) ($100-300)

Classic cab: C3.1.2, mask painted grill and head lights

C3.1.3 This variation occurred just as production resumed in 1945 or 1946. The cab retains both the open wheel-well and the low hitch; however, the tires have changed to a smooth, black synthetic rubber material. This is a relatively scarce variation and appears to have been produced for only a short time prior to the redesign of the hitch. Since this toy is between fifty and sixty years old, finding this variation in a mint state is somewhat challenging. This variety is seen only in Red.

R-4: Red ($10-20) ($30-60)

C3.2.1 The change in the design of the hitch and the change in the tire to synthetic rubber appear to have occurred at about the same time. This variation retains the open wheel-well, but has the "high" hitch and black tires. It is assumed that production of this variation began at the same time or shortly after production resumed in 1945 and continued for several years. Given Barclay's tendency to overlap production of different variations, it is possible that some pieces of the low hitch variety continued to be produced even as the high hitch varieties were being introduced. This variety is seen relatively often, however, true mint specimens are elusive. This variation comes only in Red.

R-2: Red ($10-15) ($20-30)

Classic cabs: C3.2.1 and C3.2.2, high hitch and open wheel-wells

C3.2.2 This variation has open wheel-wells, a high hitch, and white rubber tires. This variety was probably produced in the transition period when production resumed after World War II and reflects the desire to use up any remaining inventory of the white rubber tires. This variation is seen in Red only and is scarce.

R-4: Red ($15-20) ($30-60)

C3.3 This type features black synthetic tires and a high hitch; however, the mold has been changed to create half-open or, depending upon your point of view, half-closed wheel-wells. It is not known whether this was done to simplify the manufacturing process or to strengthen the wheel assembly. In any case, this appears to be a relatively short-lived experiment and examples of this type are somewhat scarce. Reflecting continued reworking of the molds, the half-open wheel-well variety only has partial lettering of the manufacturer and country of origin. It is assumed that this type was produced around 1950, immediately before closing the wheel-well altogether. This variation exists in both Red and Light Green with Red being by far the most common.

R-3: Red ($10-15) ($20-30)
R-5: Light Green ($25-35) ($40-60)

Classic cabs undersides: closed wheel-well and half-open wheel-well

C3.4.1 This is the final major type seen in the Third Series cab. This cab retains the high hitch and the smooth black synthetic tires; however, the wheel-well is now completely closed. This is by far the most commonly seen Third Series cab. While most specimens show wear from play, mint specimens are relatively common. It is assumed that production of this variation began in the early 1950s and continued through approximately 1965. Virtually all examples of this type are in Red; however, Green is occasionally encountered. In the late 1950s through 1965, a number of color variations were introduced for very short periods. These include Dark Blue, Light Blue, Grey, Orange, and Light Pink. All of these colors are extremely scarce in all conditions.

R-1: Red ($2-4) ($5-10)
R-3: Green ($10-12) ($15-25)
R-7: Dark Blue, Light Blue, Gray, Orange, and Light Pink ($40-60) ($75-150)

Classic cab 3.4.1 colors: *back row,* Dark Blue, Red, Orange, and Gray; *front row,* Pink, Light Green, and Light Blue

C3.4.2 This is another transitional variation. This cab is the same as the C3.4.1 cab with a high hitch and closed wheel-wells; however, the tires have the same ridge as is found on the tires on the Fourth Series cabs. This is another transitional variety and suggests that production of the Third and Fourth Series of cabs may have overlapped. This variation is normally found in Red and is somewhat scarce. The Moss Green, Gray, and Salmon versions are extremely scarce.

R-2: Red ($4-8) ($10-20)
R-7: Moss Green, Gray, and Salmon ($40-60) ($75-150)

Classic cab 3.4.2 colors: Moss Green, Red, Salmon, and Gray

Classic cab C3.4.2 underside. Note ridged wheels

C3.4.3 It would seem that this variation should not exist, but it does. In this case, the cab is exactly like the C3.4.1 type except that it has white rubber wheels. The only reasonable explanation for this variety is that Barclay still had some of the white wheels left as late as the 1950s. This variation is very scarce.

R-7: Red ($30-50) ($65-85)

Classic Series Trailers

The Third or Classic Series introduced both new constructions for the trailers as well as the very popular four-car trailer. When first introduced in 1939, the Third Series continued the tradition of the First and Second Series and was offered with a two-car trailer. In this version of the transport, the trailer was cast out of lead and painted, the same material and process used for both the cab and the cars. Either at the time production resumed in 1945 or shortly thereafter, the composition and the construction of the trailer changed to stamped, unpainted metal, primarily aluminum. In the case of the cast trailers, a mint specimen should be bright and shiny on the unpainted underside. The steel axles on a mint specimen should have no rust and again be shiny.

While there are a number of variations, virtually all of the stamped metal trailers have aluminum platforms with metal connectors on the four-car versions. There are several variations of this trailer; however, the basic design continued throughout the rest of the Third Series and through the Fourth Series. Mint specimens of the aluminum trailers are obtainable; however, they are definitely less common than are used specimens. A mint trailer should almost have a mirror appearance and be free of scratches, rubs, and bends. The metal connectors, the rivets, and the axles should be free of rust and shiny. Dating is again based on a combination of memory and deduction. While it is believed that the dating is relatively accurate, virtually no records exist from Barclay Manufacturing Company and the exact dates of some of the variations may never be known. It also must be remembered that Barclay often overlapped production so some of the trailer variations may have been, and most likely were, produced simultaneously.

Scarcity and pricing is listed in italics after the detailed description for each piece. Due to variations seen in the market, prices are listed in ranges for examples in C-8 (Very Good) and C-10 (Mint) conditions.

Third or Classic Series Two-Car Trailers				Unpainted	Blue-Lt.	Orange	Yellow
2T3.1.1	(BV11)	1939-42	Cast, White Wheels, Painted				
2T3.1.2	(BV11)	1945-46	Cast, Black Wheels, Painted				
2T3.1.3	(BV11)	1945-46	Cast, Black Wheels, Painted, Reinforced Tabs				
2T3.2.1	(BV75) (330)	1945-65	Aluminum, Black Wheels				
2T3.2.2	(BV75) (330)	1945-46	Aluminum, White Wheels				
2T3.2.3	(BV75) (330)	1945-59	Copper Plated Steel, Black Wheels				
2T3.2.4	(BV75) (330)	1945-59	Steel, Black Wheels				
2T3.3	(BV75) (330) (BV107a) (330)	1965-70	Aluminum, Ridged Black Tires				
Additional Variety-Trailer-2T3.2.3 With Trailer Painted Blue							

Classic Series Two-Car Trailers

2T3.1.1 The Third Series was introduced in 1939 and produced continually until Barclay ceased toy production in April 1942. The design of the trailer differed from the first two series. First, this trailer was manufactured by the injection die-cast casting process using the same materials and processes used to manufacture the cabs and the cars. In contrast to the straight trailers of the earlier series, the trailer is bent in the middle, which brings the back of the trailer down to near ground level. The trailer is approximately three and one quarter inches long. The top, sides, front tab, and rear tab were painted; however, the bottom of the trailer was not painted. On the underside, the words "BARCLAY" and "MADE IN USA" are included in the casting. Most of the cast trailers have smooth, white, natural rubber wheels suggesting that they were produced before production ceased in the spring of 1942. The most common color is Blue followed by Yellow and Orange. For reasons that cannot be fully explained, the paint coverage on the Blue version is typically much more complete than it is on the other colors. The Yellow trailers in particular tend to have areas with less than complete paint coverage.

Two problems arose with respect to the construction of this trailer. First, there was some tendency for the trailer to split approximately at the bend in the trailer. Second, there was a significant likelihood that the tabs either would partially or completely break off. The problem with tab breakage was particularly acute with the Orange trailers. Given that these toys are now over sixty years old, it is not surprising that mint specimens are difficult to locate. This is particularly true for any color other than Blue. The paint on a mint specimen will have a high sheen, the bare metal on the underside will be bright and shiny, and the axle will be free of rust and have a newer appearance. Given Barclay's tendency to use whatever parts were available, it is possible that a small number of these trailers were produced after World War II.

R-3: Light Blue ($15-18) ($20-30)
R-4: Orange, Yellow ($20-25) ($30-50)

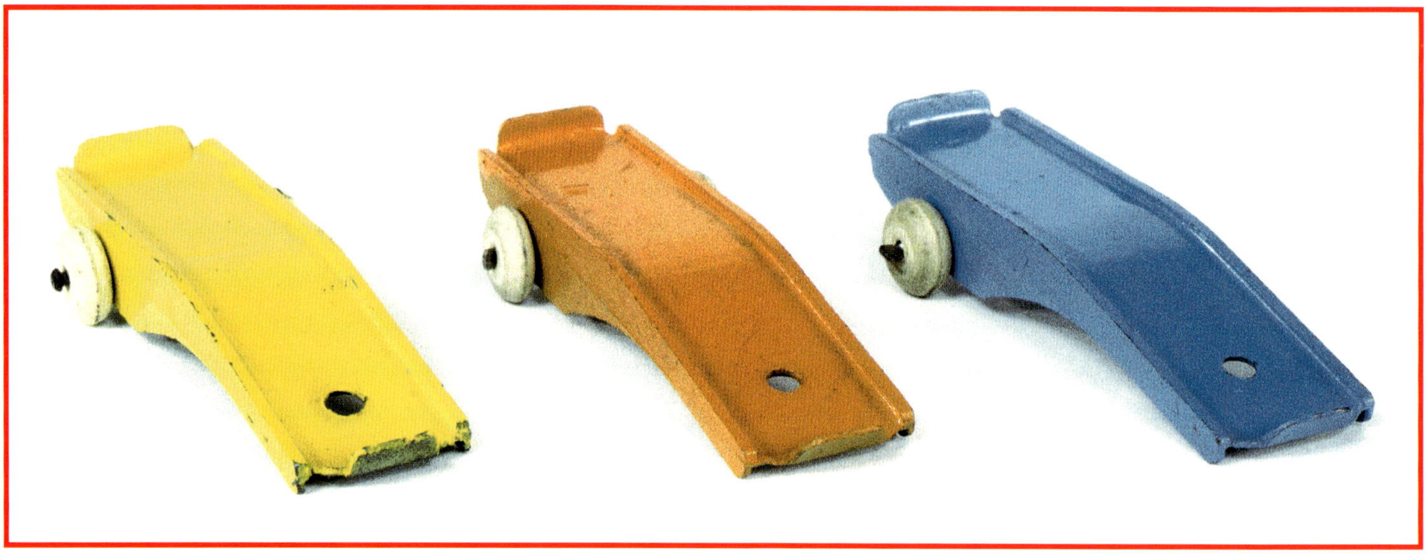

Classic trailer 2T3.1.1. Cast colors: Yellow, Orange, and Blue

Classic trailer 2T3.1.1. Cast underside. Note manufacturer's name and country of origin

2T3.1.2 This variety of the cast trailer is the same as the 2T3.1.1 trailer; however, the tires are smooth, rounded, black synthetic rubber in place of the white natural rubber tires. It is presumed that this version of the trailer was produced at the time production resumed after World War II or very shortly thereafter. This trailer is only seen in Blue and is scarce.

R-4 Light Blue ($15-20) ($30-50)

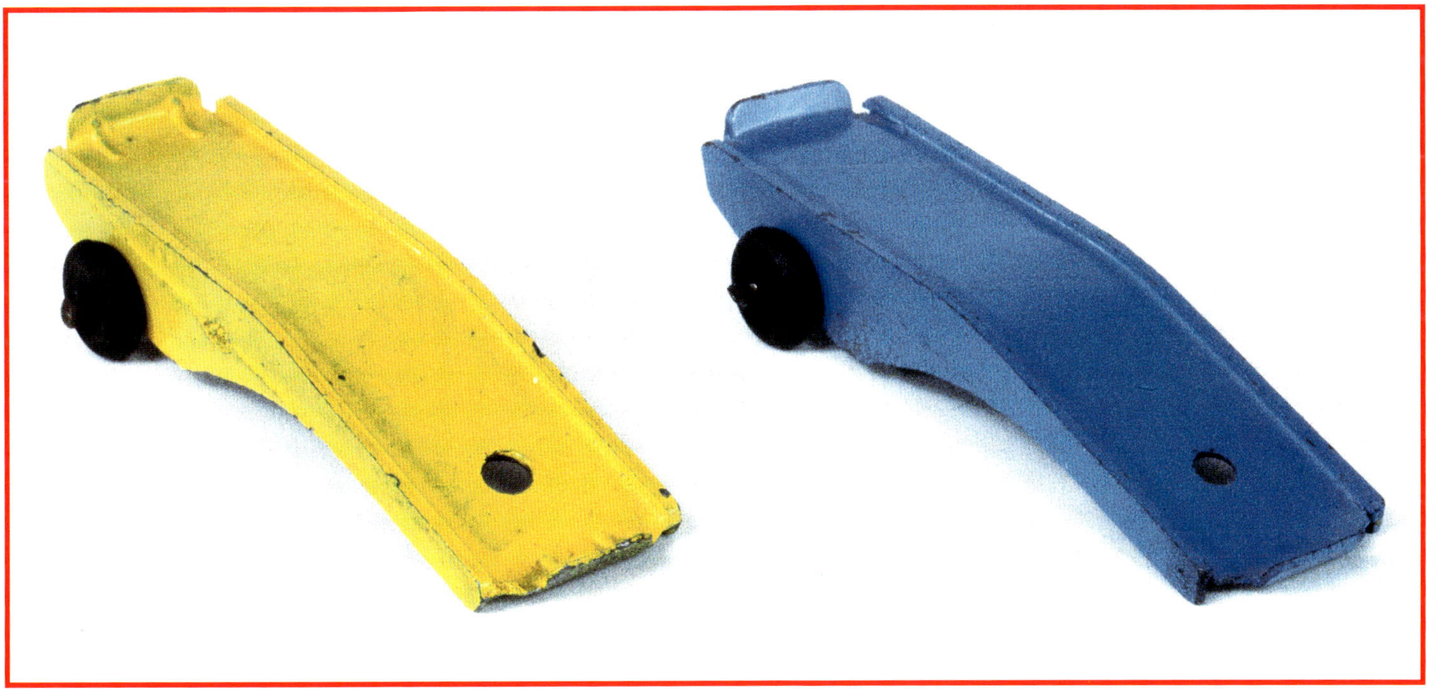

Classic trailers 2T3.1.2 and 2T3.1.3. Note reinforcement bars on the 2T3.1.3 trailer. Both have black tires

2T3.1.3 This version of the cast trailer is the same as the 2T3.1.2 variety with black synthetic rubber wheels. Barclay attempted to reinforce the front and back tabs by placing two extra bars on the upper side of each tab. While the reinforced tabs appear to have helped, the trailer is still seen with broken or partially broken tabs. The problem of spotty paint coverage of the Yellow paint also exists with this variety. Since the stamped metal trailer was introduced shortly after production resumed, this variation of the cast trailer had to have had a relatively short life and is more difficult to locate than the version with white wheels. As with the white wheel version, true mint specimens are quite difficult to locate. This trailer is only seen in Yellow.

R-4: Yellow ($15-20) ($30-50)

2T3.2.1 Shortly after resuming production of the Transport Series toys in 1945, the cast trailer was abandoned. This new trailer was stamped aluminum and was unpainted. These trailers were made for Barclay by Heyco Products, Inc., which was located in Kenilworth, New Jersey. In contrast to the cast trailers, there is no indication of either the manufacturer or the country of origin. The platform is a single piece of aluminum bent in the middle, similar to the cast trailers. This means that the back of the trailer rides close to the ground. There are tabs at each end, which are bent up to hold the cars on the trailer. The wheels are smooth, black, synthetic rubber. This trailer was used for the two-car transport set from 1945 until approximately 1965. Mint specimens are available and should have a bright, unused appearance with no scratches or marks. On a mint example, the steel axle should have no rust, the appearance should be shiny and new, and the tires should not show use.

R-1: Unpainted ($4-7) ($10-20)

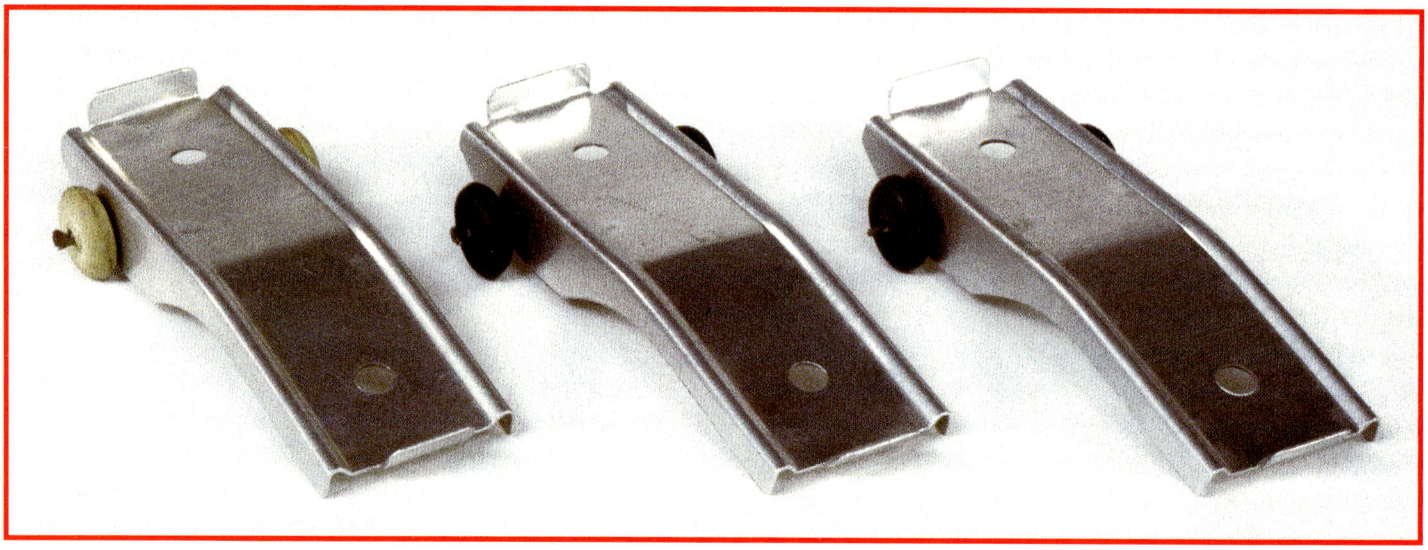

Classic trailers 2T3.2.2, 2T3.2.1, and 2T3.3. All are aluminum

2T3.2.2 This version of the two-car trailer is the same as the 2T3.2.1, except that it has the smooth, round, white rubber tires used on the earlier trailers. Whether this style was produced for a short time when production was restored or simply reflects the use of some leftover parts, we will probably never know. This version of the trailer was produced in 1945 or early 1946 and is quite scarce. As with all natural rubber tires, the tires tend to discolor and crack even on mint specimens. If tires appear to be new, bright white, and soft, they are most likely replacements.

R-5: Unpainted ($15-20) ($30-60)

2T3.2.3 This version of the two-car trailer is the same as the 2T3.2.1 type, except that the platforms are stamped from copper-plated steel. These trailers are typically seen with the older style Third Series cabs and they were manufactured sometime between 1945 and the early 1950s when Heyco purchased a company that specialized in copper-coated metals. This variety is quite difficult to locate and extremely scarce in mint condition.

R-6: ($35-45) ($55-95)

2T3.2.4 This version of the two-car trailer is also the same as the 2T3.2.1 type, except that both the platforms and the connectors are stamped from sheet steel. While it is assumed that these pieces were made in the earlier years of the Third Series, the exact date of their manufacture is not known. Another question is whether the steel trailers were all made at the same time or whether Heyco made them periodically when they ran out of the sheet aluminum or, perhaps, when they made a fortuitous purchase of sheet steel. While not as scarce as the copper trailers, they are difficult to locate, particularly without rust, and extremely scarce in mint condi-

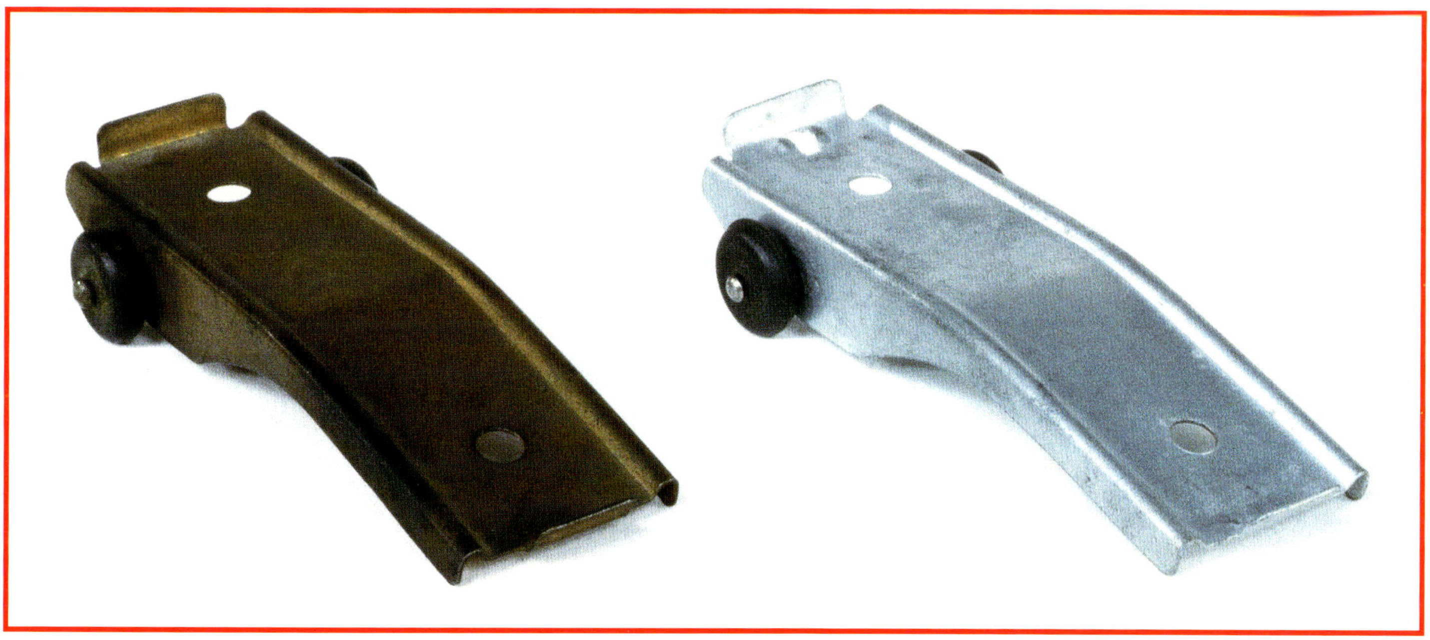

Classic trailers 2T3.2.3 and 2T3.2.4. Copper-plated steel and steel

tion. It is safe to assume that the steel trailers were manufactured sometime between 1945 and 1959, with the earlier part of this period being the most likely date.

A variation of this trailer exists with white rubber tires and the top surface painted a blue color very similar to the color used to paint the cast trailers in the Classic series. It is not known whether a trailer of this type was actually sold or whether this was simply a prototype.

R-6: Unpainted ($15-20) ($30-50)

2T3.3 This final version of the two-car trailer in the Third Series era is the same as the 2T3.2.1; however, the tires have a ridge in the middle of the tire where the tire touches the ground. The ridged tire is in contrast to the smooth round tires that had previously been used. The ridged tires were introduced on the Fourth Series Cabs in 1965 or 1966; however, the C3.4.2 cab also has ridged tires. At least a small number of Third Series sets had the C3.4.2 cab and the 2T3.3 trailer. This trailer continued to be manufactured until 1969 or 1970 as part of all of the Fourth Series two-car sets. This trailer is available in the better conditions; however, Fourth Series sets are seen far less frequently than sets of the Third Series.

R-2: Unpainted ($4-7) ($10-15)

Scarcity and pricing is listed in italics after the detailed description for each piece. Due to variations seen in the market, prices are listed in ranges for examples in C-8 (Very Good) and C-10 (Mint) conditions.

Third or Classic Series Four-Car Trailers				Unpainted
4T3.1.1	(BV157) (440)	1945-64	Aluminum, Smooth Black Wheels, Tab Hole, Separate Steel or Aluminum Tab in Place	
4T3.1.2	(BV157) (440)	1945-46	Same as 4T3.1.1, But Smooth White Tires	
4T3.1.3	(BV157) (440)	1945-59	Same as 4T3.1.1, But Copper Plated Steel	
4T3.1.4	(BV157) (440)	1945-59	Same as 4T3.1.1, But Steel	
4T3.1.5	(BV157) (440)	1960s	Aluminum, Smooth Black Wheels, Tab Hole with Lower Tab Unbent and Scoring Across the Tab	
4T3.1.6.1	(BV157) (440)	1960s	Aluminum, Smooth Black Wheels, Tab Hole with Lower Tab Bent Up, No Separate Tab or Scoring	
4T3.1.6.2	(BV157) (440)	1960s	Aluminum, Smooth Black Wheels, Tab Hole with Lower Tab Bent Up, No Separate Tab or Scoring, Tap Hole on Upper Platform	
4T3.1.7	(BV157) (440)	1960s	Same as 4T3.1.1, But Ridged Tires	
4T3.2.1	(BV157) (440) (BV107) (440)	1965-70	Aluminum, No Tab Hole, Back Tab Bent Up, Ridged Black Tires	
4T3.2.2	(BV157) (440) (BV107) (440)	1965-70	Aluminum, No Tab Hole, Back Tab Not Bent Up, Ridged Black Tires	
Additional Variety-4T3.2.2 Axle With Nub at Both Ends				

Classic Series Four-Car Trailers

4T3.1.1 Either at the time production resumed in 1945 or shortly thereafter, Barclay introduced its extremely popular four-car transport. These trailers were also made for Barclay by Heyco Products. In contrast to the cast trailers, there is no indication of either the manufacturer or the country of origin. This trailer has an upper and lower platform made from stamped aluminum. The platforms are connected with two connecters or riggers normally made from stamped galvanized steel. The steel connectors are attached to the upper platform with hollow brass rivets. An axle holding two smooth, rounded, black synthetic rubber tires is attached to the lower platform. The platform riggers are held to the lower platform by means of the axle.

Each of the platforms is bent in the middle like the platform for the two-car transport. The upper platform has tabs bent up at each end to hold the cars on the platform. The lower platform has a tab bent up in front; however, in the back there is an unbent tab. The fact that the back tab is not bent up allows the cars to be rolled off the lower trailer. In order to keep the cars on the transport, there is a small hole at the back of the lower platform that holds a separate, detachable tab. This detachable tab is a very small piece made from either aluminum or steel. Since this piece is frequently lost, many trailers of this type have the straight tab bent up in order to keep the cars on the trailer. With variations, this was the basic design of the four-car trailer throughout the Third and Fourth Series. Mint specimens are available and should have a bright, unused appearance with no scratches or marks. The axle and the connectors are steel, should have no rust, and should have a shiny, new appearance. The tires should not show use. This particular version of the trailer was produced continuously from 1945 through the mid-1960s, when a variation with ridged tires appeared.

R-1: Unpainted ($15-20) ($25-45)

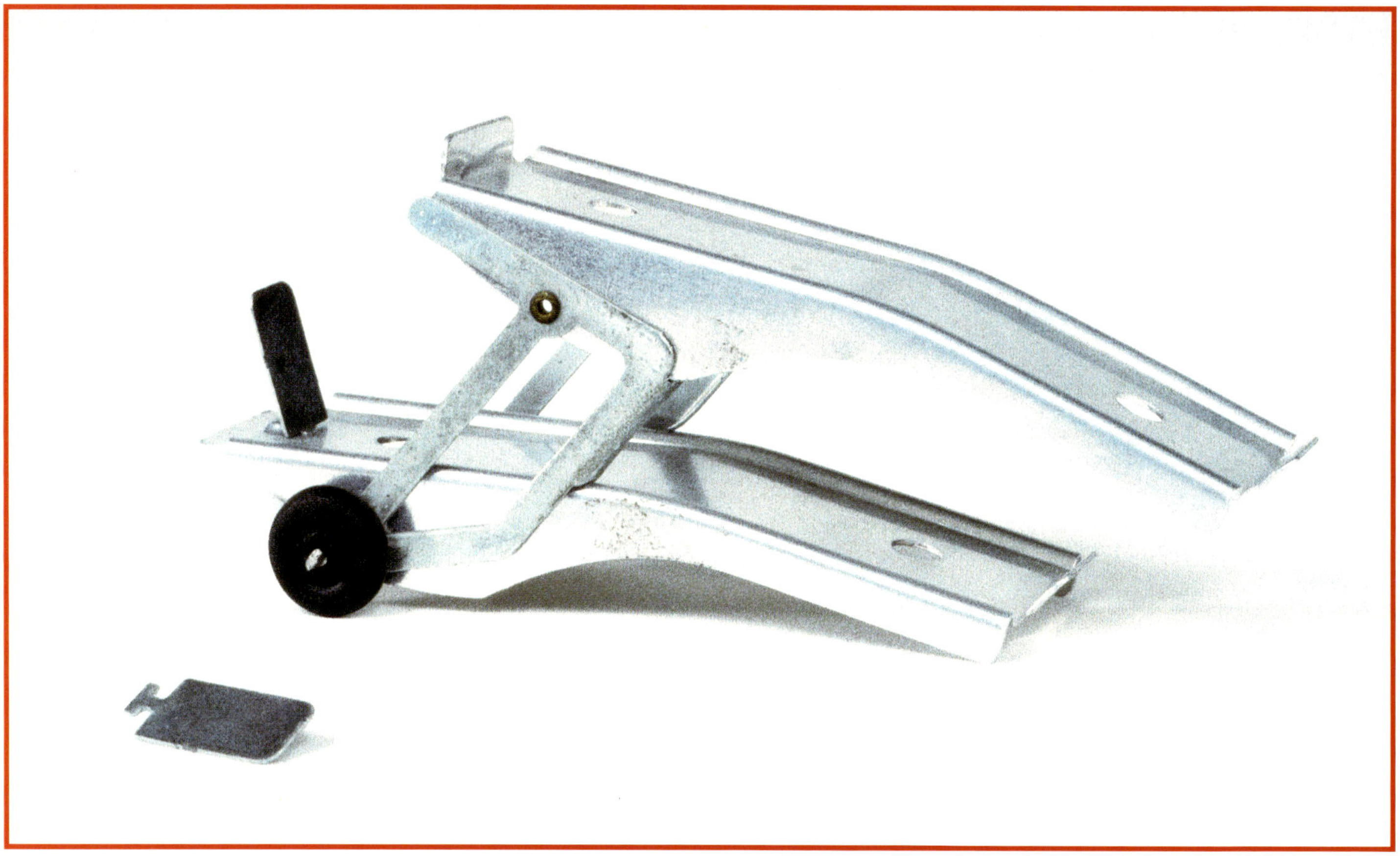

Classic trailer 4T3.1.1. Aluminum, showing removable tab

4T3.1.2 This version of the four-car trailer is the same as the 4T3.1.1 trailer, except that it has the smooth, round, white rubber tires used on the earlier cast trailers. Whether this style was produced for a short time when production was restored or simply reflects the use of some leftover parts, we will probably never know. This version of the trailer is quite scarce. As with all natural rubber tires, the tires tend to discolor and crack even on mint specimens. If tires appear to be new, bright white, and soft, they are most likely replacements.

R-5: Unpainted ($30-40) ($50-80)

4T3.1.3 This version of the four-car trailer is the same as the 4T3.1.1 trailer, except that both the platforms and the connectors are stamped from copper-plated steel. These trailers are typically seen with the older style Third Series cabs and they were manufactured sometime between 1945 and the early 1950s when Heyco purchased a company that specialized in copper-coated steel. They are quite difficult to locate and are extremely scarce in mint condition.

R-6: Unpainted ($40-50) ($60-100)

4T3.1.4 This version of the two-car trailer is also the same as the 4T3.2.1, except that both the platforms and the connectors are stamped from sheet steel. While it is assumed that these pieces were made in the earlier years of the Third Series, the exact date of their manufacture is not known. Another question is whether the steel trailers were all made at the same time or whether Heyco made them periodically, when they ran out of the sheet aluminum or, perhaps, when they made a fortuitous purchase of sheet steel. While not as scarce as the copper trailers, they are difficult to locate, particularly without rust, and extremely scarce in mint condition. It is safe to assume that the steel trailers were manufactured sometime between 1945 and 1959, with the earlier part of this time period being the most likely date.

R-5: Unpainted ($25-35) ($50-80)

4T3.1.5 This variation of the basic four-car trailer is similar to the 4T3.1.1 variety. It has the hole on the lower platform for the detachable tab; however, the straight tab that extends from the platform was scored with the intention that the customer could then bend the tab up. It is not clear whether the detachable tab was included in these sets or not, however, it most likely was not. We know that the basic 4T3.1.1 trailer continued into the earlier years of the bubble pact packaging; therefore, it is assumed that the scored-tab trailers were manufactured in the early 1960s. This version of the trailer is available; however, it is clearly scarcer than most versions of the four-car trailer.

R-4: Unpainted ($20-30) ($40-70)

4T3.1.6.1 This variation of the four-car trailer is similar to the 4T3.1.1 variety. There is a hole on the lower platform for the detachable tab; however, there is no detachable tab. The straight tab that extends from the lower platform is not scored; however, this tab is bent up to hold the cars on the lower trailer. The difficulty in identifying this variation is that many of the detachable tabs for the older trailers were lost and their owners bent up the lower back tab. The crease for the tabs bent at the factory is very straight and even and is at exactly the same angle as the upper back tab. This variation occurred in the early 1960s.

R-2: Unpainted ($15-20) ($30-40)

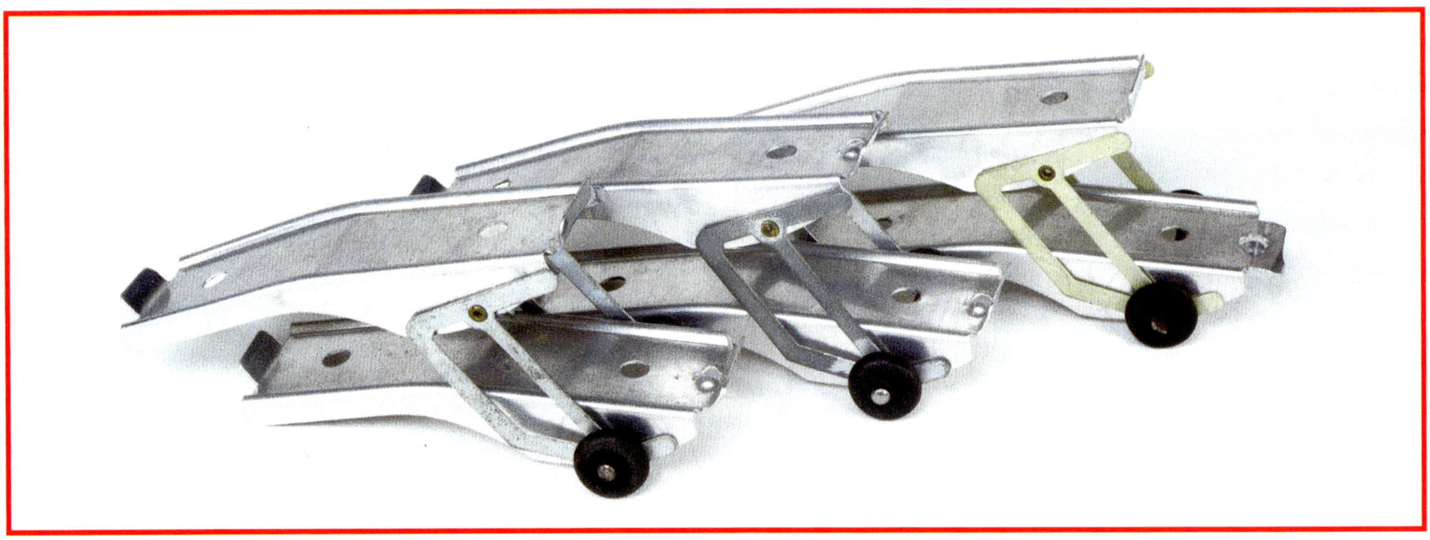

Classic trailers 4T3.1.6.1 (hole in lower platform, but tab bent up), 4T3.1.6.2 (upper platform has tab hole), 4T3.1.5 (scored tab)

4T3.1.6.2 This minor version of 4T.1.6.1 is the same as that version except that the upper platform has a tab hole like the lower platform. This variation also occurred in the early 1960s.

R-4: Unpainted ($20-30) ($40-50)

4T3.1.7 This variation is the same as the 4T3.1.1 except that the tires are the "ribbed" variety seen on the later versions of the trailer as well as on the Fourth Series cabs. This variation is somewhat scarce and may have been manufactured simultaneously with the 4T3.2.1 and/or 4T3.2.2 trailers.

R-5: Unpainted ($25-35) ($50-70)

4T3.2.1 This type of the four-car trailer is the same as the 4T3.1.1 except that the tab hole for the detachable tab has been removed and the tab extending from the back of the lower platform is bent up. The tires are ridged. As with the earlier trailers, if the tab was bent at the factory the crease will be very straight, very tight to the platform, and at the same angle as the upper trailer. The 4T3.2.2 trailers frequently had their back bent up by their owners. Typically, the inexactness of the bend is obvious; however, they are sometimes confused with the 4T3.2.1 trailers.

At least a small number of sets containing this variation of the four-car trailer were issued with the Third Series cabs; however,

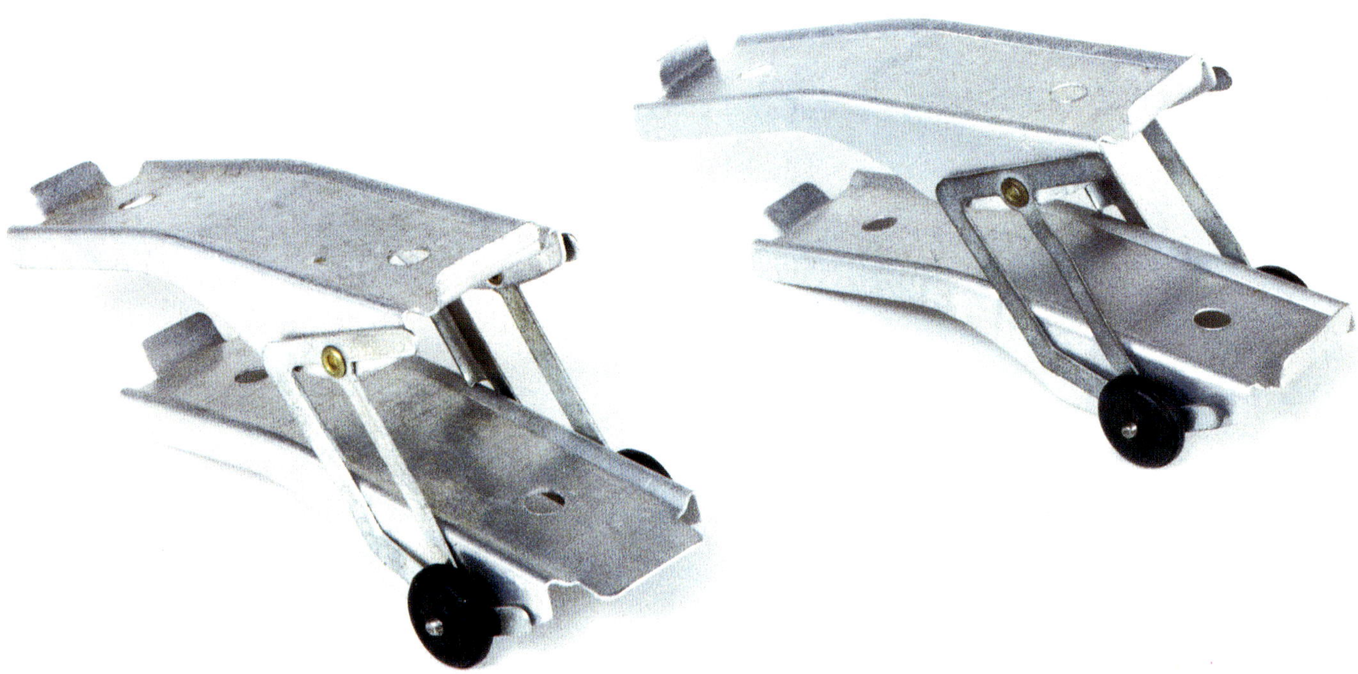

Trailers 4T3.2.1 (no tab hole, tab bent up) and
4T3.2.2 (no tab hole, straight tab). Note ribbed tires

this trailer is primarily seen as part of the Fourth Series trailer sets. This variation appeared at the very end of the Third Series; therefore, it dates from 1964 or 1965 and ended in 1969 or 1970. This trailer variation appears to have been produced both at the beginning of the Fourth Series as well as nearer the end. The 4T3.2.2 trailer, to be discussed in a moment, was definitely produced between 1963 and 1970. It is certainly possible that the 4T3.2.1 trailer was produced simultaneously with the 4T3.2.2 variation. These trailers overlapped the Third and Fourth Series of cars. Sets from the early to mid-1960s contained various combinations of the Third and Fourth series cars.

R-2: Unpainted ($10-15) ($20-40)

4T3.2.2 This variation of the four-car trailer is the same as the 4T3.2.1 trailer except that the tab extending from the back of the lower platform is not bent. Owners frequently bent the tab up; however, any attempt to bend the tab detracts from the value of the piece. As noted, this variation is generally seen in sets that can be dated in the middle of the 1963-1970 period. It may have been produced exclusively for a period of time or simultaneously with the 4T3.2.1. It appears that this variation of the four-car trailer was only used with the Fourth Series cabs and cars. While this variation is available, it is seen less frequently than its companion 4T3.2.1 trailer.

A variation of this variety exists with a nub at both ends of the axle.

R-2: Unpainted ($15-20) ($25-45)

Classic Series Cars

Like the cars in the First and Second Series, the cars in the Third or Classic Series come in two varieties, sedans and coupes. All of the cars were cast using the injection die-cast casting method. Normally, the one-piece cast body was spray-painted and the metal wheels were then attached by means of a steel axle. As will be explained, very early in the production of this series of cars, Barclay apparently experimented with painting the cars after the axles were attached. This appears to have been a very short-lived experiment.

The axle is a pin with a nub at one end and a crimp at the other end. These cars have open side windows and you can expect to see a minor amount of paint splashed on the inside.

The Classic Series design was introduced in 1939 and was produced continuously until approximately 1965. The Fourth Series cars or "Shoebox" cars were introduced in the very late 1950s or the early 1960s and were produced simultaneously with the Third Series cars for several years. Unlike the earlier cars, the Third Series cars come in a number of distinct variations and a substantial number of colors, which changed over time. In respect to the colors, we have identified the major variations. Barclay did not scientifically mix their paints and you will find slight shade and tint variations throughout the series. While it is expected that mint specimens be free from chipping, it is not unusual to see a mint specimen with chips that it received while being manufactured, packed, and shipped.

There is debate in respect to the number of molds that were used to produce the cars in the Third Series. The memory of some of the older Barclay workers is that each mold produced two to four cars. Given the fact that different variations exist and that they

Classic sedans

Classic coupes

were produced at the same time in some cases and at different times in others, it is assumed that multiple molds were used for various periods of production.

Scarcity and pricing is listed in italics after the detailed description for each piece. Due to variations seen in the market, prices are listed in ranges for examples in C-8 (Very Good) and C-10 (Mint) conditions.

Third or Classic Series Sedans (440 or 330)			**Blue-Lt.**	**Blue**	**Camel**	**Chocolate**	**Clay**	**Flesh**	**Gray**	**Green-Forest**	**Green-Lt.**	**Green-Moss**	**Orange**	**Pink**	**Red**	**Salmon**	**Silver**	**Tan**	**Yellow**	**Yellow-Lemon**
Plain Sedans																				
S3.1.1	1939-50s	Cast, Plain Grill, Open Wheel-Wells, Unpainted Metal Wheels, Two Door Handles, Perhaps '39 Buick	X	X						X	X		X						X	
S3.1.2	1939	Same as 3.1.1 Except Painted Wheels	X								X								X	
S3.1.3	1950s-65	Same as 3.1.1 Except Closed Wheel-Wells	X	X	X	X	X		X	X	X	X	X	X	X	X	X	X	X	X
S3.1.4.1	1957-65	Same as 3.1.1 Except Gold Colored Wheels								X										
S3.1.4.2	1957-65	Same as 3.1.3 Except Gold Colored Wheels						X		X	X		X		X					
S3.1.5	1965	Same as 3.1.3 Except Dull Cleated Rubber Tires								X			X							
Parking Light Sedan																				
S3.2.1	1939	Cast, Plain Grill, Open Wheel-Wells, Unpainted Metal Wheels, Sq. Parking Light Left Front, Die Cut Left Back, Two Door Handles Dipping Wind Shield, Flat Headlights									X		X						X	
S3.2.2	1939-50s	Same as 3.2.1 Except Painted Wheels									X									
S3.2.3	1950s-65	Same as 3.2.1 Except Closed Wheel-Wells	X	X	X		X		X		X	X	X	X	X	X	X		X	
S3.2.4	1965	Same as 3.2.3 Except Dull Cleated Rubber Tires									X									
Grill Bars Sedan																				
S3.3	1950s-65	Cast, Vertical Grill, Closed Wheel-Wells, Metal Wheels, Four Door Handles, Partial Left Front Parking Light Rounded Trunk	X	X	X				X		X	X	X	X	X	X	X		X	

Additional Varieties:
S3.1.3 Double Painted. Light Blue Over Orange
S3.1.2 The Only Known Lt. Green Example Is Painted Solid Green Inside
S3.1.2 The Only Known Blue Example Is Painted Yellow Inside and Then Over Painted Blue On The Outside

Classic Series Sedans

S3.1.1 Plain Sedan As seen in the accompanying pictures, this car is cast with a plain grill, open wheel-wells, unpainted metal wheels, and two door handles. The car has the appearance of a 1939 Buick. This variation was first produced in 1939 and production continued until the 1950s, when the wheel-wells were closed. This variation is the most available of the earlier Third Series sedans; however, mint specimens of this earlier type are more difficult to locate than the later variation with closed wheel-wells. Certain colors are quite scarce, particularly in mint condition. Mint specimens should have complete and vibrant paint, the inside of the casting and the wheels should be bright and shiny, and the axle should be free from rust and should have a silvery appearance.

The most common colors in the open wheel-well variety of the Plain Sedan are Light Green and Orange. These colors were offered throughout the production of this variation. The remaining colors are not rare, but definitely more scarce.

R-2: Light Green, Orange ($8-12) ($15-20)
R-3: Light Blue, Blue, Forest Green, and Yellow ($10-15) ($20-25)

Classic Plain Sedans, S3.1.1 and S3.1.3

Classic cars undersides, closed wheel-well and open wheel-well

Drawing of Classic Plain Sedan

S3.1.2 Plain Sedan This variation is the same as the S3.1.1 except that the casting was painted before the wheels were attached resulting in wheels that are painted the same color as the body. It is almost certain that these cars were produced in 1939 and they are extremely scarce in all colors. They should not be confused with cars that were painted later outside of the factory.

R-6: All Colors ($25-30) ($40-80)

Classic sedans and coupes, S3.1.2, CO3.1.2, and Modern sedan, all with painted wheels

S3.1.3 Plain Sedan This variation is the same as the S3.1.1 sedan except that the wheel-wells have been closed. It was produced from the 1950s until the end of the Third Series in 1965.

This is clearly the most available of the Third Series sedans; however, certain colors are quite scarce, particularly in mint condition.

R-1: Light Green and Orange ($8) ($10-20)
R-2: Light Blue, Blue, Camel, Forest Green, Red, and Silver ($10-12) ($15-25)
R-3: Pink, Tan, and Yellow ($12-15) ($20-30)
R-6: Clay, Moss Green, Gray, Salmon, Lemon Yellow ($35-40) ($50-100)
R-7/10: Chocolate (Only one example known)

S3.1.4.1 and S3.1.4.2 Plain Sedan These variations are the same as the S3.1.1 and S3.1.3 Plain Sedans; however, the silver colored metal wheels are replaced with gold colored wheels. It is not absolutely certain when these cars were produced, but it appears to be in the transition period when the Third and Fourth Series cars were being produced together because this "gold wheel" variation is often found with a mixture of Third and Fourth Series cars with gold colored wheels. This would place production of this variation in the late 1950s or early 1960s, most likely near the end of this period. This variation is very scarce and difficult to locate. It is not clear how an open wheel-well example of this variety could exist except the possible existence of older castings that were completed several years after the casting was originally made.

R-6: All Colors except Flesh ($20-25) ($30-70)
R-7/10: Flesh (Only on example known)

Classic and Modern cars with gold wheels. Note stamped price on car to left

S3.1.5 Plain Sedan This variation is also the same as the S3.1.3 sedans; however, the wheels are the dull rubber wheels with cleats found on the Fourth Series cars that were manufactured beginning approximately 1965. This transitional variety was most likely produced just as production of the Third Series cars ceased. This variety is rare in all colors and very difficult to locate.

R-7: All Colors ($35-40) ($50-100)

Classic Plain Sedan S3.1.5. Dull rubber wheels

S3.2.1 Parking Light Sedan This variation is similar to the Plain Sedan. The piece has a plain grill, open wheel-wells, unpainted metal wheels, and two door handles. Once again, it resembles a 1939 Buick. The Parking Light Sedan has two distinctive features, a small square parking light on the left front fender and a die cut on the left back fender. For some collectors, the most distinctive element of this variety is the straight headlights found on this variety in contrast to the rounded headlights found on the Plain Sedans. Since the wheel-well is open, this variation was produced in the earlier years of the production of the Third Series. Whether it was produced at the very start of production is not clear. Since there is a distinct contrast between this car and the Plain Sedan, it is assumed that this variety was produced from a separate mold.

In general, this variation is scarcer than the Plain Sedans, particularly in mint condition, and more difficult to locate than the later variation of Parking Light Sedans with closed wheel-wells. The most common colors are Light Green and Orange. Yellow is relatively scarce.

R-3: Light Green and Orange ($15-18) ($20-35)
R-5: Yellow ($20-25) ($35-45)

Classic Parking Light Sedans. Note parking light on front left fender and die cut on left back fender

Drawing of Classic Parking Light Sedan

S3.2.2 Parking Light Sedan This version of the Parking Light Sedan is exactly the same as the S3.2.1, however, this early version of the Parking Light Sedan was painted after the wheels were attached producing a car with wheels painted exactly the same color as the car. As previously noted, this variation was almost certainly produced in 1939 and may have been an experiment. In any case, these cars are rare in all colors and should not be confused with cars that were painted outside the Barclay factory.

R-7: All Colors ($35-40) ($50-100)

S3.2.3 Parking Light Sedan This variation of the Parking Light Sedan is the same as the S3.2.1 except that the wheel-wells are closed. Production of this type began in the early to mid 1950s and continued until production of the Third Series stopped in the mid-1960s. While this variation is the most common of the Parking Light Sedans, it is definitely more difficult to locate than the Plain Sedan and in certain colors is extremely scarce. The most common colors are Light Green and Orange.

R-3: Light Green and Orange ($10-15) ($20-25)
R-5: Light Blue, Blue, Camel, Pink, Red, Silver, and Yellow ($20-25) ($35-45)
R-7: Moss Green, Gray, and Salmon ($40-50) ($65-95)
R-7/10: Clay (Only one example known)

S3.2.4 Parking Light Sedan This variation is also the same as the S3.2.1 sedans; however, the wheels are the dull rubber wheels with cleats found on the Fourth Series cars beginning approximately 1965. This transitional variety was most likely produced just as production of the Third Series cars ceased. This variety is rare in all colors and very difficult to locate.

R-7: All Colors ($35-40) ($50-100)

S3.3 Grill Bars Sedan This type of sedan clearly differs from other variations. Since it has closed wheel-wells, it is assumed that production began sometime in or after the early to mid 1950s. Production continued until the production of the Third Series cars ceased about 1965. The car is similar to the Plain Sedan; however, it has three very distinct features and a fourth more subtle difference. First, on each side of the front grill, this sedan has three vertical grill bars. Second, in contrast to the other sedans in the Third Series, this version has four door handles. Third, it has a small parking light on the left front fender. Fourth, the body of this sedan is slightly narrower than either the Plain or Parking Light Sedans.

Classic Grill Bars Sedan. Note four door handles and set of bars on front grill

While the Grill Bars Sedan can be located, it is definitely more difficult to find than either the Plain Sedan or the Parking Light Sedan. The only colors encountered with any frequency are Light Green and Orange. All other colors vary from very scarce to rare.

Drawing of Classic Grill Bars Sedan

R-3: Light Green and Orange ($15-20) ($25-30)
R-5: Light Blue, Blue, Camel, Pink, Red, Silver, and Yellow ($25-30) ($40-50)
R-7: Moss Green, Gray, and Salmon ($45-55) ($75-105)

Scarcity and pricing is listed in italics after the detailed description for each piece. Due to variations seen in the market, prices are listed in ranges for examples in C-8 (Very Good) and C-10 (Mint) conditions.

Third or Classic Series Coupes (440 or 330)			Blue-Lt.	Blue	Brown	Camel	Clay	Cream	Flesh	Gray	Green-Forest	Green-Lt.	Green-Moss	Magenta	Orange	Pink	Red	Salmon	Silver	Tan	Yellow	Yellow-Lemon
Plain Coupes																						
CO3.1.1	1939-50s	Cast, Wide Body, Open Wheel-Wells, Unpainted Metal Wheels, Full Grill, Smooth Cast, Wide Body Perhaps '39 Plymouth	■	■							■	■					■				■	
CO3.1.2	1939	Same as 3.1.1 Except Painted Wheels															■					
CO3.1.3	1950s-65	Same as 3.1.1 Except Closed Wheel-Wells	■	■	■		■	■		■	■	■	■	■	■	■	■	■	■	■		■
CO3.1.4	1957-65	Same as 3.1.3 Except Gold Colored Wheels	■						■			■			■		■					
CO3.1.5	1965	Same as 3.1.3 Except Dull Cleated Rubber Tires		■											■		■		■			
Crooked Line Coupe																						
CO3.2.1	1950s-65	Cast, Narrow Body, Closed Wheel-Wells, Metal Wheels, Crooked Line on Right Grill, Tapered Backend Perhaps '37 Willys or '37 Studebaker	■	■	■					■		■	■		■	■	■	■				
CO3.2.2	1957-65	Same as 3.2.1 Except Gold Wheels										■					■					
No-Line Coupe																						
CO3.3	1950s-65	Cast, Mid-Width Body, Closed Wheel-Wells, Metal Wheels, Headlight and Three Grill Bars on Left Side, No Headlight and One Grill Bar on Right Side, Later Version had no Headlight or Grill on Left Side, Rounded Backend	■	■	■	■				■		■	■		■	■	■	■				
Additional Variety:																						
CO3.1.3		Double Painted. Light Green Over Pink																				

Classic Series Coupes

CO3.1.1 Plain Coupe As seen in the accompanying pictures, this car is cast with a full grill, wide body, open wheel-wells, and unpainted wheels. This variety has the appearance of a 1939 Plymouth. This variation was first produced in 1939 and production continued until the 1950s, when the wheel-wells were closed. This variation is the most available of the earlier Third Series coupes; however, mint specimens of this earlier type are more difficult to locate than the later variation with closed wheel-wells. Certain colors are quite scarce, particularly in mint condition. Mint specimens should have complete and vibrant paint. The inside of the casting and the wheels should be bright and shiny. The axle should be free from rust and should have a silvery appearance. Blue and Red are the most common colors. Other colors are scarce.

R-2: Blue and Red ($10-12) ($15-20)
R-3: Light Blue ($12-15) ($20-25)
R-4: Light Green ($15-20) ($25-35)
R-5: Forest Green ($20-25) ($30-40)
R-7/10: Yellow (Only one example known)

Classic Plain Coupes, CO3.1.1 and CO3.1.3

CO3.1.2 Plain Coupe This variation is exactly like the CO3.1.1 except that the casting was painted before the wheels were attached resulting in wheels that are painted the same color as the body. It is almost certain that these cars were produced in 1939. These cars are extremely scarce in all colors and they should not be confused with cars that were painted later outside of the factory.

R-6: All Colors ($25-35) ($40-80)

CO3.1.3 Plain Coupe This variation is the same as the CO3.1.1 coupe except that the wheel-wells have been closed. It was produced from the early 1950s until the end of the Third Series, about 1965. This is clearly the most available of the Third Series Coupes; however, certain of the colors are scarce to extremely rare, particularly in mint condition.

R-1: Blue and Red ($8) ($10-20)
R-2: Light Blue ($10-12) ($15-25)
R-3: Forest Green, Light Green, Orange, Pink, and Silver ($12-15) ($20-30)
R-5: Cream, Salmon, Tan, and Lemon Yellow ($20-25) ($30-40)
R-6: Moss Green and Gray ($35-40) ($50-80)
R-7/10: Brown, Clay, and Magenta (Only one example of each known)

Drawing of Classic Plain Coupe

CO3.1.4 Plain Coupe This variation is the same as the CO3.1.3 coupe; however, the silver colored metal wheels were replaced with gold colored wheels. It is not certain when these cars were produced, but it was first seen in the transition period when the Third and Fourth Series cars were being produced together. The "gold wheel" variation is often found with a mixture of Third and Fourth Series cars with gold colored wheels. This would place production of this variation in the late 1950s to the mid 1960s, most likely near the end of this period. This variation is very scarce and difficult to locate.

R-6: All Colors except Flesh ($20-25) ($30-70)
R-7-10: Flesh (Only one example known)

CO3.1.5 Plain Coupe This variation is also the same as the CO3.1.3 coupes; however, the metal wheels are the dull rubber wheels with cleats found on the Fourth Series cars beginning approximately 1965 or 1966. This leads us to conclude that this is another transitional variety produced just as production of the Third Series cars ceased. This variety is extremely scarce and very difficult to locate in all colors.

R-7: All Colors ($35-40) ($50-100)

CO3.2.1 Crooked-Line Coupe On first glance, this variation is similar to the Plain Coupe; however, on closer inspection, it is clearly from a different mold. The body is distinctly narrower than the Plain Coupe and has a Crooked-Line cast into the right side of the grill. Aside from the narrow body, this variety can be distinguished from the No-Line variety by the way the rear end peaks in the middle and then tapers down toward each side in contrast to the rounded rear end of the No-Line variety. Some believe that this car resembles either a 1937 Willys or a 1937 Studebaker. Since the wheel-well is closed, this variation was first produced in the 1950s.

Classic Crooked-Line Coupes. Note tapered roofs

The wheels on this variety were attached after the car was painted, resulting in unpainted wheels. This variety is available; however, it is definitely scarcer than the Plain Coupe and, in some colors, it is very scarce. The most common colors are Blue, Pink, and Red. All other colors are very scarce to rare.

R-3: Blue, Pink, and Red ($10-15) ($20-25)
R-5: Light Blue, Light Green, Orange, and Salmon ($20-25) ($35-45)
R-6: Moss Green and Gray ($40-50) ($65-95)
R-7/10: Brown (Only one example known)

Drawing of Classic Crooked-Line Coupe

CO3.2.2 Crooked-Line Coupe This version of the Crooked-Line Coupe is the same as the CO3.2.1; however, the silver colored metal wheels were replaced with gold colored wheels. It is not certain when these cars were produced, but they were first seen in the transition period when the Third and Fourth Series cars were being produced together. The "gold wheel" variation is often found with a mixture of Third and Fourth Series cars with gold colored wheels. This would place production of this variation in the late 1950s to mid 1960s period, most likely near the end of this period. This variation is very scarce and difficult to locate.

R-6: All Colors ($25-35) ($40-85)

CO3.3 No-Line Coupe This type of coupe is clearly distinct from the other variations. Since it has closed wheel-wells, it is assumed that production began sometime around 1950 and continued until the production of the Third Series cars ceased about 1965. This car has a wider body than the Crooked-Line Coupe, but a slightly more narrow body than the Plain Coupe; a headlight and three grill bars on the left side; and no headlight and one grill bar on the right side. A later version has no headlight or grill on either side. The easiest way to differentiate the No-Line Coupe from the Crooked-Line Coupe is that the rear end of the No-Line Coupe is rounded in contrast to the Crooked-Line Coupe, where the rear end peaks in the middle and then tapers to each side. While the No-Line Coupe can be located, it is definitely more difficult to find than the Plain Coupe or the Crooked-Line Coupe.

R-3: Blue and Red ($15-20) ($25-30)
R-5: Light Blue, Camel, Light Green, Orange, Pink, Salmon, ($25-30) ($40-50)
R-7: Moss Green, and Gray ($45-55) ($75-105)
R-7/10: Brown (Only one example known)

Classic No-Line Coupe

Drawing of Classic No-Line Coupe

Classic Series Original Sets

Original sets are made up of pieces of similar age and condition. In general, a matched original set is more difficult to locate than a set that combines pieces from multiple sources, which may vary in age and condition. A two-car set typically consists of a cab, trailer, sedan, and coupe. Most four-car sets were sold with a cab, trailer, two sedans, and two coupes. Perhaps as early as the late 1950s and certainly in the 1960s, some four-car sets were sold with varying combinations of sedans and coups. One set might have three sedans and one coupe, while the next set might have three coupes and one sedan. Below is listed the correct combinations for the various classic sets. While Barclay may have mixed various pieces when they were available, these are the standard combinations by cab type. Pricing is for a set with the most common pieces.

C3.1.1 or C3.1.2 with 2T3.1.1 White wheeled, open wheel-well cab with painted, white-wheeled trailer and open wheel-well cars.

R-3: Matched Set ($45-60) ($70-90)

C3.1.3 with 2T3.1.2 or 2T3.1.3 Black wheeled, open wheel-well cab with painted, black-wheeled trailer and open wheel-well cars.

R-4: Matched Set ($50-65) ($75-95)

C3.2.1 with 2T3.2.1, 2T3.2.3, 2T3.2.4, 4T3.1.1, 4T3.1.3, 4T3.1.4, 4T3.1.5, 4T3.1.6.1, or 4T3.1.6.2 Black wheeled, high hitch, open wheel-well cabs with trailers of period and open wheel-well cars.

R-3: Matched Two-Car Set ($35-40) ($45-60)
R-3: Matched Four-Car Set ($80-110) ($115-125)
R-5: Matched Four-Car Set in Box (Mint Only) ($140-200)

C3.2.2 or C3.4.3 with 2T3.2.2 or 4T3.1.2 White wheeled, high hitch, open wheel-well cabs with corresponding trailers.

R-6: Matched Two-Car Set ($55-65) ($85-110)
R-6: Matched Four-Car Set ($95-120) ($140-240)

C3.3 or C3.4.1 with 2T3.2.1, 2T3.2.3, 2T3.2.4, 4T3.1.1, 4T3.1.3, 4T3.1.4, 4T3.1.5, 4T3.1.6.1, or 4T3.1.6.2 Half open or closed wheel-well cab with period trailers and closed wheel-well cars.

R-2: Matched Two-Car Set ($35-40) ($40-55)
R-5: Matched Two-Car Set in Bubble Pack (Mint Only) ($60-75)
R-2: Matched Four-Car Set ($75-100) ($110-120)
R-5: Matched Four-Car Set in Box (Mint Only) ($135-195)
R-5: Matched Four-Car Set in Bubble Pack (Mint Only) ($100-115)

C3.4.2 with 2T3.3, 4T3.1.7, 4T3.2.1, or 4T3.2.2 Ridged tired cabs and trailers with closed wheel-well cars.

R-2: Matched Two-Car Set ($35-40) ($40-55)
R-5: Matched Two-Car Set in Bubble Pack (Mint Only) ($60-75)
R-2: Matched Four-Car Set ($75-90) ($95-100)
R-5: Matched Four-Car Set in Bubble Pack (Mint Only) ($100-115)

Various combinations of Classic and Modern Series cars exist in bubble packs with seven (7) cars to the set. Packs with all Classic cars command the highest prices. No price is given for packs containing rare variations and colors.

R-5: Various Combinations of Seven Cars in a Bubble Pack (Mint Only) ($60-$120)

Classic Series: Other Characteristics, Packaging, and Availability

The Classic Series is the most widely recognized and the most widely collected of the four Barclay Transport Series. The Classic Series includes a tremendous number of variations as well as the most common and the rarest pieces found in the various series. Since the cars were sold individually as well as part of the sets, there are many more cars than there are cabs and trailers. For reasons that are not clear, there also appear to be more cabs than there are trailers.

Classic 4-car trailer set

While many Classic Series pieces come to the collectible toy market, original sets are relatively scarce. Many of the sets that are offered are in fact mismatched combinations of cabs, trailers, and cars that simply were never sold together. While the earlier open wheel-well varieties are seldom distinguished in the market, many of these pieces are much more difficult to find than are the later varieties. As collectors become more aware of the variations, these earlier varieties will undoubtedly gain the interest that they deserve.

As has been indicated, this series was sold as individual cars, sets of cars, two-car trailer sets, and four-car trailer sets. As far as it is known, the four-car trailer sets were first sold as a boxed set. At least some of the earlier two-car sets were sold attached to a flat piece of cardboard, but it is not known whether this packaging method was consistently used or not. The cars were sold during the 1950s as individual pieces without packaging and were probably shipped in bulk. Beginning in the late 1950s or early 1960s, the cars, two-car trailer sets, and four-car trailer sets began to be sold in bubble packs. Throughout the life of the Third Series, the most common color combination in the four-car sets was a Green and an Orange sedan paired with a Blue and a Red coupe.

While many pieces of the Third Series are available in the collectors' market, the pieces most frequently encountered are the more common varieties and colors in grades less than C-10. There are numerous varieties within this series that are very difficult to find and that range from scarce to extremely rare.

Classic Plain Sedans. Originally painted Orange, but over-painted in Light Blue

Detailed Catalog: Fourth or Modern Series

The Fourth or Modern Series of Barclay Auto Transports was the final chapter in this extended line of toys. The cars and the cabs are distinctly different from those of the Third Series. Even though this series is not as old as the Third Series, the Third Series is seen much more frequently. Since none of the pieces in the Modern Series are identified by either manufacturer or country of origin, they are often misattributed to other manufacturers. The transition from the Third or Classic Series to the Modern Series actually took place over several years. The Modern Series cars, which are also call "Shoebox" cars, were introduced either at the very end of the 1950s or the very early 1960s. These cars were produced simultaneously with the Classic Series cars until about 1965 or 1966.

The Modern Series cabs were introduced about 1965 and continued until Barclay ceased production in 1971. Fourth Series had both two-car and four-car transport sets and was sold in sets of the

Modern 2-car and 4-car trailer sets

cab, transport, and matching cars as well as in sets of cars only. At least a limited number of cars were sold individually. In contrast to the Third Series, there is limited variation in terms of the castings; however, there are a number of variations in terms of the materials used and substantial varieties of color. In this section, we will systematically discuss and illustrate each of the known varieties.

Modern Series Colors

Initially, the cars in the Modern Series were produced simultaneously with the cars of the Classic Series and used the same colors. With minor changes, these colors continued throughout most of the production period for the Modern Series. In contrast to the Classic Series, the colors are consistent and you see relatively few shade variations.

Modern colors, first set: Aqua, Black, Blue, Light Blue, and Light Brown

Modern colors, first set: Steel Blue, Flesh, Clay, Cream, and Forest Green

In the last year or two before Barclay ceased operations, the color range was substantially expanded to include new, bright and hot colors. During this period, most of the traditional colors continued to be produced. Many of the colors in this final version of the Fourth Series are quite difficult to locate.

Modern colors, first set: Light Green, Metallic Green, Gray, Orange, and Orange-Hot

Modern colors, first set: Burnt Orange, Pink, Bright Pink, Red, and Red-Hot

Modern colors, first set: Silver, Salmon, Tan, Yellow, and Lemon Yellow

Scarcity and pricing is listed in italics after the detailed description for each piece. Due to variations seen in the market, prices are listed in ranges for examples in C-8 (Very Good) and C-10 (Mint) conditions.

Fourth or Modern Series Cabs				Blue-Hot	Blue-Dk.	Green-Forest	Orange	Orange-Red Hot	Pink-Hot	Red	Salmon	Yellow-Hot
C 4.1	(BV107a or 107) (330 or 440)	1966-70	Cast, Black Wheels, '63 Ford									
C 4.2	(BV107a or 107) (330 or 440)	1970-71	Cast, Black Wheels with White Sidewalls, '63 Ford									

Modern Series Cabs

The Fourth Series cab is a modern cab over engine design patterned after a 1963 Ford semi-trailer cab. The cab is almost exactly two and one-quarter inches in length, one and one-eighth inches in width at its widest point, and one and one-quarter inches in height. The profile is definitely higher than the Third Series cabs; however, this cab pulls the same trailers as the Third Series cabs. As with the previous series, this cab was cast by forcing hot metal into a bronze mold under pressure using the injection die-casting method. The casting was then spray-painted and the axles and wheels were attached. The cab has open windows; therefore, it should have at least some traces of the paint on the inside. There is no identification on the casting; therefore, it is often misattributed to other manufacturers.

Although the Modern Series Cab was the last cab to be made, it is more difficult to locate than the cabs from the Classic Series, particularly in pristine, mint condition. Generally, the paint on the Modern Series cabs covers very well; however, there are often paint chips on the more pronounced edges of the cab, even on pieces that are near mint. The inside of the cab should be shiny and the axles should be rust free on a mint specimen. The Modern Series cab was introduced in 1965 or 1966; several years after the Shoebox cars were introduced. Except for one minor variation and differences in color, the Modern cab continued until Barclay ceased production in 1971.

C4.1 The Fourth Series or Modern Series cab pulls both the two-car and four-car trailers. While the basic construction of the cab is the same as the Classic Series cab, the wheels are the synthetic rubber with a ridge running around the middle of the tire. These tires are the same as the tires on the last version of the Classic Series cab. Virtually all examples of this cab are painted Red; however, Dark Blue, Orange, and Salmon specimens exist and are very scarce. This version of the Modern Series cab was first produced from approximately 1965 or 1966 and continued to be produced until 1969 or 1970. Given Barclay's tendency to overlap both series and variations, it is very possible that this variation was produced until Barclay closed in 1971.

R-1: Red ($3-4) ($5-10)
R-6: Dark Blue, Orange, and Salmon ($30-40) ($50-80)

Modern cab C4.1, Salmon, Dark Blue, and Red

C4.2 This type of the Modern Series cab was produced just before Barclay's closure. The first production probably took place in 1969 or 1970 and it was produced until Barclay ceased production in 1971. This cab is the same as the C4.1 cab except that wheels have a white circle painted around the outside of the tire to give the wheel the appearance of a whitewall. We do not know the reason for having a whitewall on a truck. Aside from the colors of Red and Dark Blue from the C4.1 cab, this cab also comes in Hot

Blue, Forest Green, Hot Orange-Red, Hot Pink, and Hot Yellow. All whitewall cabs of this type are scarce and many of the colors are extremely scarce.

R-6: All Colors ($30-50) ($50-100)

Modern cab C4.2, Hot Orange-Red, Dark Blue, Forest Green, and Red. Note white sidewall tires

Modern Series Trailers

Until the whitewall version of the trailer was introduced in 1969 or 1970, the Modern Series used the trailers from the last years of the Classic Series. Specifically, the two-car transport sets used the 2T3.3 trailer with the ridged tire and the four-car transport sets used either the 4T3.2.1 or the 4T3.2.2 trailer. The Modern Transport four-car set was introduced in approximately 1965. For reasons that cannot be explained, the 4T3.2.1 trailer with the bent up lower back tab seems to have been the norm both in the earlier years and in the final years of production. The 4T3.2.2 with the straight, unbent tab seems to have been used between these two periods. It is also quite possible that both varieties were produced simultaneously.

Scarcity and pricing is listed in italics after the detailed description for each piece. Due to variations seen in the market, prices are listed in ranges for examples in C-8 (Very Good) and C-10 (Mint) conditions.

Fourth or Modern Series Two-Car Trailers					Unpainted
2T4.1	(BV107a)	(330)	1965-70	Same as 2T3.3	
2T4.2	(BV107a)	(330)	1970-71	Same as 2T3.3 with White Sidewalls	

Modern Series Two-Car Trailers

2T4.1 This trailer is the same as the 2T3.3 trailer.

R-2: Unpainted ($4-7) ($10-15)

2T4.2 This trailer is the same as the 2T3.3 trailer except that it has whitewall tires as discussed in the previous section on the Modern Series cabs. All trailers with whitewall tires are quite scarce.

R-6: Unpainted ($25-30) ($40-80)

Scarcity and pricing is listed in italics after the detailed description for each piece. Due to variations seen in the market, prices are listed in ranges for examples in C-8 (Very Good) and C-10 (Mint) conditions.

Fourth or Modern Series Four-Car Trailers					Unpainted
4T4.1	(BV107)	(440)	1965-70	Same as 4T3.2.1	
4T4.2	(BV107)	(440)	1965-70	Same as 4T3.2.2	
4T4.3	(BV107)	(440)	1970-71	Same as 4T3.2.1 with White Sidewalls	

Modern Series Four-Car Trailers

4T4.1 This trailer is the same as the 4T3.2.1 trailer.

R-2: Unpainted ($10-15) ($20-40)

4T4.2 This trailer is the same as the 4T3.2.2 trailer.

R-2: Unpainted ($15-20) ($25-45)

4T4.3 This trailer is the same as the 4T3.2.2 trailer except that it has white walls. Trailers of this type are quite scarce.

R-6: Unpainted ($30-40) ($50-100)

Modern Series Cars

Production of the Fourth or Modern Series cars began in either the late 1950s or very early 1960s. The cars of this series are known as "Shoebox" cars due to their shape. While the designs are decidedly more modern than the cars in the Classic Series, they also are much less detailed. The Shoebox cars were made in two styles, a coupe and a sedan. Some collectors suggest that they were perhaps modeled after the 1951 Packard. Both the sedans and the coupes are approximately one and nine-sixteenths inches long.

The construction of the Modern Series cars is similar to the cars in the previous series; the cast body of the car was made by injecting molten metal into a bronze die-cast mold. The completed casting was then ejected from the mold by a series of ejector pins. After the casting was created, the cars were spray-painted and finally the steel axles were inserted and the wheels were attached. Until about 1965 when the Modern Series cab was introduced, the Shoebox cars were produced simultaneously with the Classic Series cars. They were frequently found in all three bubble packs of this era, typically mixed with cars from the Classic Series. At least a few of the Modern Series cars were sold individually by retailers in a similar manner to the cars in the Classic Series.

As with all Barclay vehicles of this period, mint specimens should not have chips, should be bright and shiny on the inside, should be free of rust on the axles, and the axles should have minimal discoloration. Since these cars have open windows, there should be some paint splashed on the inside having come through the windows as the car was painted. There are a number of different varieties of Fourth Series cars. Variations resulted from changes in the molds, changes in the tires, and numerous variations of color. There is no manufacturer or country of origin identified; therefore, Shoebox cars are often misattributed to other manufacturers.

One unique characteristic of the Shoebox cars is a number from one to eight on the inside of the roof of each car. It is assumed that this number identifies a specific mold or a position within in the mold; however, this cannot be conclusively proven. In terms of scarcity, cars in true mint state are more difficult to find than one might assume due to the tendency of the cars to easily chip and the ebbing popularity of Barclay products as the 1960s progressed.

The most common cars are the first type with metal wheels. The varieties produced after 1965 are generally more difficult to locate and some colors and some styles are extremely difficult to find. This last statement is particularly true of the final style produced for a short period immediately before Barclay's shutdown. It should be noted that the quality of the cars gradually deteriorated through the latter part of the 1960s and on into 1970 and 1971.

Note on Scarcity and Pricing of all Modern Series Cars: *In general the collectors' market has not recognized the relative scarcity of the Modern Series Cars. The steel-wheeled variation is the most common variety. Throughout the series, the most common colors are Blue, Light Green, Orange, and Red. The authors believe that their color listings are relatively complete; however, they also believe additional color varieties exist within some of the type variations. Scarcity and pricing is listed in italics after the detailed description for each piece. Due to variations seen in the market, prices are listed in ranges for examples in C-8 (Very Good) and C-10 (Mint) conditions.*

Fourth or Modern Series Sedans (440, 330, or 331)		Black	Blue	Blue-Lt.	Flesh	Brown-Lt.	Chocolate-Metallic	Clay	Cream	Gray	Green-Forest	Green-Lt.	Orange	Orange-Hot	Pink	Pink-Bright	Purple	Red	Silver	Tan	Yellow	Yellow-Lemon
S4.1.1	1957-65 Cast, Metal Wheels and Axles, Marked 1-8, Open Back Window, Eyelet Axle Holder Perhaps '51 Parkard																					
S4.1.2	1960-65 Same as S4.1.1 Except Gold Wheels																					
S4.2.1.1	1965-66 Same as S4.1.1 Except Cleated Rubber or Plastic Vinyl Tires, Metal Axle made from Pin Crimped at One End, Forked or Eyelet Wheel Assembly, Open Back Window																					
S4.2.1.2	1965-66 Same as S4.2.1.1 Except Closed Back Window																					
S4.2.2.1	1966-70 Same as S4.2.1.1 Except Axle Nub-Both Ends																					
S4.2.2.2	1966-70 Same as S4.2.1.2 Except Axle Nub-Both Ends																					
S4.2.3	1966-70 Same as S4.2.1.2 Except with Small Smooth Rubber Tires, Metal Axle made from Pin Crimped at One End, Forked Axle Holders, Closed Back Window																					
Additional Variety: S4.1.1 Blue with Painted Tires																						

Modern Series Sedans

S4.1.1 This Shoebox sedan has metal wheels and axles, has the numbers one through eight marked on its roof, has an open back window, and has eyelet axle holders. This type was most likely first produced in the late 1950s and its production continued until about 1965. This is the oldest and most common Shoebox car, although certain colors are relatively scarce. An interesting aspect of this sedan is that it was produced simultaneously with the Classic Series sedan and the sedans of the two series were often mixed together in car and trailer sets. This practice continued until the Modern Series trailer sets were introduced around 1965. As far as is known, this version of the Shoebox car was not used on the Modern Series trailer sets.

R-1: Blue, Light Green, Orange, and Red ($2-3) ($4-7)
R-2/R-4: All Other Colors except Clay ($4-5) ($5-15)
R-6: Clay ($15-25) ($30-50)

Modern cars underside, eyelet axle holder

Modern sedan S4.1.1, steel wheels

S4.1.2 This variation is the same as S4.1.1 except that it has gold colored metal wheels rather than the more common silver colored metal wheels. This variety is often seen with the gold-wheeled variety of the Third Series cars; therefore, it is assumed that these cars were produced in the first half of the 1960s when both types were being produced simultaneously. This variety is very scarce.

R-6: All Colors ($20-25) ($30-70)

Modern cars S4.1.2 and CO4.1.3, gold wheels

S4.2.1.1 This is the second type of Shoebox car. The body of the car is essentially the same as the S4.1.1 type; however, the wheels are made from either a dull, synthetic rubber or plastic vinyl. Both types of wheels have cleats. The two wheel varieties are difficult to differentiate; however, the rubber variety tends to be more flexible and appear dull when compared to the plastic variety. In contrast, the plastic wheels are relatively stiff and tend to have a shiny appearance. There are two varieties of the wheel assembly. The more common version has a forked axle holder. A second version has the eyelet axle holder used on the S4.1.1 variety. The axle is steel made from a metal pin with a nub at one end and a crimp at the other end. The back window is open. This version of the Shoebox car appears to have been made from about 1965 until the final version was introduced around 1969 or 1970. While available, this variety is not nearly as common as the earlier cars with metal wheels and is challenging to collect in its various sub-varieties.

R-2/R-4: All Colors ($3-8) ($5-20)

Modern sedans, rubber or plastic tires

S4.2.1.2 This variation of the Shoebox car is the same as the S4.2.1.1 car; however, it has a closed rear window. As previously noted, it is not known whether the closed rear window variation was the result of a faulty manufacturing process or was produced from molds that were slightly different. This variation is more difficult to locate than the open window variety.

R-2/R-4: All Colors ($3-8) ($5-20)

S4.2.2.1 This variation is the same as the S4.2.1.1 with an open rear window; however, the axle has a nub at both ends. It is not known when this variety was produced, but it was during the 1966 to 1970 period. It is distinctly possible that this variation was produced simultaneously with other variations and it is relatively difficult to locate.

R-2/R-4: All Colors ($5-10) ($10-25)

Modern sedans and coupes with double nub on axles

S4.2.2.2 This variation is the same as the S4.2.1.2 with a closed rear window; however, the axle has a nub at both ends. It is not known when this variety was produced, but it was during the 1966 to 1970 period. It is distinctly possible that this variation was produced simultaneously with other variations and it is relatively difficult to locate.

R-2/R-4: All Colors ($5-10) ($10-25)

S4.2.3 This variation of the Shoebox car is the same as the S4.2.1.1 except that the wheels have a small, smooth synthetic rubber tire. The car has a steel axle made from a pin with a nub at one end and a crimp at the other end, forked axle holders, and a closed back window. It is not clear when this variation was produced; however, it would have been sometime between 1966 and 1970. It is distinctly possible that this variation was produced simultaneously with other variations. This variety is relatively difficult to locate.

R-2/R-4: All Colors ($5-10) ($10-25)

Modern sedan S4.2.3. Note small, smooth, synthetic rubber tires

Scarcity and pricing is listed in italics after the detailed description for each piece. Due to variations seen in the market, prices are listed in ranges for examples in C-8 (Very Good) and C-10 (Mint) conditions.

S4.3 Fourth or Modern Series Sedans **(330, 440, or 331)**	**Black**	**Blue**	**Blue-Metallic**	**Blue-Hot**	**Cinnamon-Metallic**	**Gold**	**Green-Forest**	**Green-Metallic**	**Green-Hot**	**Maroon**	**Orange**	**Orange Hot**	**Orange-Red Hot**	**Pink-Hot**	**Purple-Hot**	**Red**	**Red-Hot**	**Red-Metallic**	**Silver**	**Violet**	**White**	**Yellow**	**Yellow-Hot**	**Yellow-Lemon**
S4.3.1 1970-71 Cast, Plastic Wheels, Plastic Axles																								
S4.3.2 1970-71 Same as S4.3.1-Flower Power Label																								
Additional Varieties: Black Over Gold, Black Over Yellow																								

S4.3.1 This final variation of the Barclay Transport sedan retains the basic shape of the Shoebox cars; however, the wheels and the axle are now a single piece of molded plastic. The plastic component is simply pushed into the forked holder. From the standpoint of playability, the design is unsatisfactory. The wheels move with difficulty, if at all, and there is a tendency for the plastic piece to pop out of the holder. This variety of car also shows a general decline in the quality of the casting process as well as the quality of the application of the paint. The most distinguishing characteristic of this type is a substantial expansion of the colors to include a number of bright and "hot" colors. This variety of car was probably introduced in 1969 or 1970 and continued until Barclay ceased operations in 1971. Although available, this type is not seen as frequently as one might expect and is very to extremely scarce in many of the colors.

R-2/R-6: All Colors ($4-20) ($6-30)

Modern colors second set: Black, Blue, Hot Blue, Metallic Blue, and Metallic Cinnamon

Modern colors second set: Copper, Gold, Forest Green, Hot Green, and Metallic Green

Modern colors second set: Maroon, Orange, Hot Orange, Orange-Red, and Hot Orange-Red

Modern colors second set: Hot Pink, Hot Purple, Red, Hot Red, and Metallic Red

Modern colors second set: Silver, Violet, Yellow, Hot Yellow, Lemon Yellow, White

Modern sedans and coupes underside. Forked axle holder with single piece axle and wheel assembly

S4.3.2 This variety is exactly the same as S4.3.1 except that a "flower power" label has been placed on the top of the car. This same label can be seen on a number of Barclay products manufactured just prior to the closure of the Company. This variety is very scarce.

R-6: All Colors ($15-25) ($30-45)

Modern sedans S4.3.2, Flower Power label

Scarcity and pricing is listed in italics after the detailed description for each piece. Due to variations seen in the market, prices are listed in ranges for examples in C-8 (Very Good) and C-10 (Mint) conditions.

Fourth or Modern Series Coupes **(440, 330, or 331)**	**Aqua**	**Black**	**Blue**	**Blue-Lt.**	**Blue-Steel**	**Clay**	**Gray**	**Green-Forest**	**Green-Lt.**	**Green-Metallic**	**Gold**	**Orange**	**Orange-Burnt**	**Pink**	**Pink-Bright**	**Red**	**Red-Hot**	**Salmon**	**Silver**	**Tan**	**Yellow**	**Yellow-Lemon**
CO4.1.1 1957-65 Cast, Metal Wheels and Axles, Marked 1-8, Open Back Window, Eyelet Axle Holder Perhaps '51 Parkard																						
CO4.1.2 1957-65 Same as CO4.1.1 Except Closed Back Window																						
CO4.1.3 1960-65 Same as CO4.1.1 Except Gold Wheels																						
CO4.2.1 1965-66 Same as CO4.1.1 Except Cleated Rubber or Vinyl Plastic Tires, Metal Axle made from Pin Crimped at One End, Forked or Eyelet Wheel Assembly, Closed Back Window																						
CO4.2.2 1966-70 Same as CO4.2.1 Except Axle Nub-Both Ends																						
CO4.2.3 1966-70 Same as CO4.2.1 Except with Small Smooth Rubber Tires, Metal Axle made from Pin Crimped at One End, Forked Axle Holders, Closed Back Window																						

Modern coupe CO4.1.1, steel wheels

Modern Series Coupes

CO4.1.1 This Shoebox coupe has metal wheels and axles, has numbers one through eight marked on the inside of its roof, has an open back window, and has eyelet axle holders. This type of car was most likely first produced in the late 1950s and its production continued until about 1965. This is the oldest and most common Shoebox coupe, although certain colors are very scarce. This coupe was produced simultaneously with the cars from the later years of the Classic Series. Cars from the two series were often mixed together in the car and trailer sets of the late 1950s and the first half of the 1960s. As far as is known, this version of the Shoebox car was not used on the Modern Series trailer sets introduced about 1965.

R-1: Blue, Light Green, Orange, and Red ($2-3) ($4-7)
R-2/R-4: Light Blue, Forest Green, Pink, Bright Pink, Silver, Tan, Lemon Yellow ($4-5) ($5-15)
R-5: Salmon ($6-10) ($15-25)
R-6: Clay ($15-25) ($30-50)
R-7/R-10: Aqua and Steel Blue (Only single examples of each known)

CO4.1.2 This variation is the same as CO4.1.1 variety except that it has a closed back window. It is assumed that it was produced during the same period as the C4.1.1. It is not known whether the closed window varieties were created due to a flawed production process or whether they simply represent a variation in one or more of multiple molds. This variety is more difficult to locate than the open window variety.

R-2/R-4: All Colors except Clay ($4-5) ($5-15)
R-6: Clay ($15-25) ($30-50)

CO4.1.3 This variation is the same as CO4.1.1 except that it has gold colored metal wheels rather than the more common silver colored metal wheels. This variety is often seen with the gold-wheeled variety of the Third Series cars; therefore, it is assumed that these cars were produced in the first half of the 1960s, when both types were being produced simultaneously. This variety is very scarce.

R-6: All Colors ($20-25) ($30-70)

CO4.2.1 This is the second type of Shoebox car. The body of the car is essentially the same as the CO4.1.1 type; however, the wheels are made from either a dull, synthetic rubber with cleats or plastic vinyl with cleats. The two wheel varieties are difficult to differentiate; however, the rubber variety tends to be more flexible and appears dull when compared to the plastic variety. In contrast, the plastic wheels are relatively stiff and tend to have a shiny appearance. There are two varieties of the wheel assembly. The more common version has a forked axle holder. A second version has the eyelet axle holder used on the CO4.1.1 variety. The axle is steel and is made from a metal pin with a nub at one end and a crimp at the other end. The back window is closed. This version of the Shoebox car appears to have been made from about 1965 until the final version was introduced around 1969 or 1970. While available, this variety is not nearly as common as the earlier cars with metal wheels.

R-2/R-4: All Colors ($5-8) ($10-20)
R-7/R-10 Steel Blue and Gray (Only one known example of each color)

Modern sedans, rubber or plastic tires

CO4.2.2 This variation is the same as the CO4.2.1 with a closed back window; however, the axle has a nub at both ends. It is not known when this variety was produced, but it was during the 1966 to 1970 period. It is distinctly possible that this variation was produced simultaneously with other variations and it is relatively difficult to locate.

R-2/R-4: All Colors ($5-10) ($10-25)

CO4.2.3 This variation of the Shoebox car is the same as the CO4.2.1 except the wheels have a small, smooth synthetic rubber tire. The car has a steel axle made from a metal pin with a nub at one end and a crimp at the other end, forked axle holders, and an open back window. It is not clear when this variation was produced; however, it was sometime between 1966 and 1970. It is distinctly possible that this variation was produced simultaneously with other variations. As compared to some of the other non-steel wheeled varieties of the Shoebox cars, this variation is relatively difficult to locate.

R-2/R-4: All Colors ($5-8) ($10-20)

Scarcity and pricing is listed in italics after the detailed description for each piece. Due to variations seen in the market, prices are listed in ranges for examples in C-8 (Very Good) and C-10 (Mint) conditions.

CO4.3 Fourth of Modern Series Coupes **(330, 440, or 331)**	**Black**	**Blue**	**Blue-Metallic**	**Copper**	**Gold**	**Green-Forest**	**Green-Metallic**	**Maroon**	**Orange**	**Orange-Red**	**Orange-Red Hot**	**Pink-Hot**	**Purple-Hot**	**Red**	**Red-Hot**	**Red-Metallic**	**Silver**	**White**	**Yellow**	**Yellow-Hot**
CO4.3 1970-71 Cast, Plastic Wheels, Plastic Axles																				

CO4.3 This final variation of the Barclay transport cars retains the same basic shape as all Shoebox cars; however, the wheels and axle are now a single piece of molded plastic. The plastic component is simply pushed into the forked holder. From the standpoint of playability, the design is unsatisfactory. The wheels move with difficulty, if it all, and there is a tendency for the plastic piece to pop out. This variety also shows the general decline in the quality of the casting process as well as in the application of the paint. The most distinguishing characteristic of this variety is a substantial expansion of the colors to include a number of bright and "hot" colors. This type of car was probably introduced in 1969 or 1970 and continued until Barclay ceased operations in 1971. Although available, this type is not seen as frequently as one might expect and is very to extremely scarce in many of the colors.

R-2/R-6: All Colors ($4-20) ($6-30)

Modern Series Original Sets

Original sets are made up of pieces of similar age and condition. As far as is known, the Modern Cab was only sold with the ridged wheel trailers and with various sets of plastic or rubber wheeled cars. In general, the trailer sets always contained a cab, trailer, and either two or four cars. Normally, the two-car trailer sets had a sedan and a coupe, while the four-car trailer sets had two sedans and two coupes. Today, pieces from the Modern Series are often mixed with pieces from the Classic Series in ways that simply never existed. The correct combinations are listed below, however, one note of caution relates to the cabs and trailers with white sidewalls. The sets in bubble pacts that have been located all include white sidewalls on both the cab and the trailer. It is possible, however, that some of the white sidewall pieces were sold with a plain sidewall companion piece. Pricing is for a set with the most common pieces.

C4.1 with 2T4.1, 4T4.1, or 4T4.2 Ridged tired cabs and trailers with matching Modern Series plastic or rubber wheeled cars.

R-2: Matched Two-Car Set ($20-25) ($30-35)
R-5: Matched Two-Car Set in Bubble Pack (Mint Only) ($40-50)
R-2: Matched Four-Car Set ($45-60) ($70-80)
R-5: Matched Four-Car Set in Bubble Pack (Mint Only) ($70-85)

C4.2 with 2T4.2 or 4T4.3 trailers and a combination of S4.3 and CO4.3 cars.

R-6: Matched Two-Car Set ($75-90) ($100-150)
R-6: Matched Two-Car Set in Bubble Park (Mint Only) ($100-150)
R-6: Matched Four-Car Set ($80-100) ($120-180)
R-6: Matched Four-Car Set in Bubble Pack (Mint Only) ($120-180)

Modern Series cars were sold in bubble packs with seven (7) cars to the set. Prices are for common variations and colors.

R-5: Seven Cars in a Bubble Pack (Mint Only) ($40-$60)

Modern Series: Other Characteristics, Packaging, and Availability

The Modern Series was the last of the four major types of Barclay Auto Transports. While it does not include the extreme rarities found in the Classic Series, overall it is clearly not as common as the Classic Series. Since the cars were sold individually as well as part of sets, there are more cars than there are cabs and trailers. As with the Classic Series, there also appear to be more cabs than there are trailers. We have identified the color variations with each type that are known; however, there is every expectation that additional colors exist within the type variations.

Except for a few cars that were apparently sold individually, virtually all of the Modern Series pieces were sold as part of bubble pack sets. It is likely that a few of the early metal-wheeled cars were mixed into the last of the boxed Classic Series sets. The different

Modern sedan S4.3.1, Black paint over Gold paint

varieties of bubble packs had sets of cars, two-car trailer sets, or four-car trailer sets. As with the Classic Series, the most common color combination in the four-car sets was a Green and an Orange sedan paired with a Blue and a Red coupe.

While many pieces of the Fourth Series are available in the collectors' market, the pieces most frequently encountered are the more common varieties and colors in grades less than C-10. There are numerous varieties within this series that are very difficult to find and that range from scarce to extremely scarce, if not extremely rare. Given their tendency for chipping, locating mint specimens of Shoebox cars is always challenging.

A Resting Place for Barclay Auto Transport Toys

Robert Wagner's Barclay junk yard

Detailed Type Listings

First or Vintage Series (Cabs, Trailers, Sedans, and Coupes)				Green	Orange	Red	Yellow
C1	(BV152)	1932-37	Cast, White Wheels, Red Hubs, Model A Ford	■		■	
2T1	(BV152)	1932-37	Steel, White Wheels, Red Hubs, Painted	■		■	
S1	(BV152 or 114)	1932-38	Cast, Metal Wheels, Closed Windows		■		■
S2	(BV152 or 114)	1932-38	Cast, Metal Wheels, Open Windows		■		
CO1	(BV152 or 114)	1932-38	Cast, Metal Wheels, Closed Windows	■		■	
CO2	(BV152 or 114)	1932-38	Cast, Metal Wheels, Open Windows			■	

Second or Streamlined Series (Cabs and Trailers)				Blue	Green	Red
C2	(BV114)	1938	Cast, White Wheels, No Hubs, "Trailer" on Side			
2T2	(BV114)	1938	Steel, White Wheels, No Hubs, Painted			
Related Variety-Cab-C2 in Red with Built-up Hitch, Not Considered as Part of this Series						
Additional Variety-Cab and Trailer with Red Hubs						

Third or Classic Series Cabs				Blue	Blue-Lt.	Green-Lt.	Green-Moss	Gray	Orange	Pink-Lt	Red	Salmon
C3.1.1	(BV11)	1939-42	Cast, White Tires, Open Wheel-Wells, Low Hitch, '38 Ford Cab Over Engine									
C3.1.2	(BV11)	1939-40	Same as C3.1.1, Except Lights and Grill Mask Painted Silver									
C3.1.3	(BV75 or 157)	1945-46	Same as C3.1.1, Except Black Tires									
C3.2.1	(BV75 or 157)	1945-49	Cast, Black Wheels, Open Wheel-Wells, High Hitch, '38 Ford Cab Over Engine									
C3.2.2	(BV75 or 157)	1945-46	Same as C3.2.1, Except White Tires									
C3.3	(BV75 or 157)	1950	Cast, Black Wheels, Half Open Wheel-Wells, High Hitch, '38 Ford Cab Over Engine									
C3.4.1	(BV75 or 157) (330 or 440)	1950-65	Cast, Black Wheels, Closed Wheel-Wells, High Hitch, '38 Ford Cab Over Engine, Smooth Wheels									
C3.4.2	(BV75 or 157) (330 or 440)	1965	Same as C3.4.1, Except Ridged Wheels									
C3.4.3	(BV75 or 157) (330 or 440)	1950-65	Same as C3.4.1, Except White Rubber Wheels									

Third or Classic Series Two-Car Trailers				Unpainted	Blue-Lt.	Orange	Yellow
2T3.1.1	(BV11)	1939-42	Cast, White Wheels, Painted				
2T3.1.2	(BV11)	1945-46	Cast, Black Wheels, Painted				
2T3.1.3	(BV11)	1945-46	Cast, Black Wheels, Painted, Reinforced Tabs				
2T3.2.1	(BV75) (330)	1945-65	Aluminum, Black Wheels				
2T3.2.2	(BV75) (330)	1945-46	Aluminum, White Wheels				
2T3.2.3	(BV75) (330)	1945-59	Copper Plated Steel, Black Wheels				
2T3.2.4	(BV75) (330)	1945-59	Steel, Black Wheels				
2T3.3	(BV75) (330) (BV107a) (330)	1965-70	Aluminum, Ridged Black Tires				
Additional Variety-Trailer-2T3.2.3 With Trailer Painted Blue							

Third or Classic Series Four-Car Trailers				Unpainted
4T3.1.1	(BV157) (440)	1945-64	Aluminum, Smooth Black Wheels, Tab Hole, Separate Steel or Aluminum Tab in Place	
4T3.1.2	(BV157) (440)	1945-46	Same as 4T3.1.1, But Smooth White Tires	
4T3.1.3	(BV157) (440)	1945-59	Same as 4T3.1.1, But Copper Plated Steel	
4T3.1.4	(BV157) (440)	1945-59	Same as 4T3.1.1, But Steel	
4T3.1.5	(BV157) (440)	1960s	Aluminum, Smooth Black Wheels, Tab Hole with Lower Tab Unbent and Scoring Across the Tab	
4T3.1.6.1	(BV157) (440)	1960s	Aluminum, Smooth Black Wheels, Tab Hole with Lower Tab Bent Up, No Separate Tab or Scoring	
4T3.1.6.2	(BV157) (440)	1960s	Aluminum, Smooth Black Wheels, Tab Hole with Lower Tab Bent Up, No Separate Tab or Scoring, Tap Hole on Upper Platform	
4T3.1.7	(BV157) (440)	1960s	Same as 4T3.1.1, But Ridged Tires	
4T3.2.1	(BV157) (440) (BV107) (440)	1965-70	Aluminum, No Tab Hole, Back Tab Bent Up, Ridged Black Tires	
4T3.2.2	(BV157) (440) (BV107) (440)	1965-70	Aluminum, No Tab Hole, Back Tab Not Bent Up, Ridged Black Tires	
Additional Variety-4T3.2.2 Axle With Nub at Both Ends				

Third or Classic Series Sedans (440 or 330)			Blue-Lt.	Blue	Camel	Chocolate	Clay	Flesh	Gray	Green-Forest	Green-Lt.	Green-Moss	Orange	Pink	Red	Salmon	Silver	Tan	Yellow	Yellow-Lemon
Plain Sedans																				
S3.1.1	1939-50s	Cast, Plain Grill, Open Wheel-Wells, Unpainted Metal Wheels, Two Door Handles, Perhaps '39 Buick	■	■						■	■		■						■	
S3.1.2	1939	Same as 3.1.1 Except Painted Wheels	■								■								■	
S3.1.3	1950s-65	Same as 3.1.1 Except Closed Wheel-Wells	■	■	■	■	■		■	■	■	■	■	■	■	■	■	■	■	■
S3.1.4.1	1957-65	Same as 3.1.1 Except Gold Colored Wheels								■										
S3.1.4.2	1957-65	Same as 3.1.3 Except Gold Colored Wheels						■		■	■		■		■					
S3.1.5	1965	Same as 3.1.3 Except Dull Cleated Rubber Tires								■			■							
Parking Light Sedan																				
S3.2.1	1939	Cast, Plain Grill, Open Wheel-Wells, Unpainted Metal Wheels, Sq. Parking Light Left Front, Die Cut Left Back, Two Door Handles Dipping Wind Shield, Flat Headlights									■		■						■	
S3.2.2	1939-50s	Same as 3.2.1 Except Painted Wheels									■									
S3.2.3	1950s-65	Same as 3.2.1 Except Closed Wheel-Wells	■	■	■		■		■		■	■	■	■	■	■	■		■	
S3.2.4	1965	Same as 3.2.3 Except Dull Cleated Rubber Tires									■									
Grill Bars Sedan																				
S3.3	1950s-65	Cast, Vertical Grill, Closed Wheel-Wells, Metal Wheels, Four Door Handles, Partial Left Front Parking Light Rounded Trunk	■	■	■				■		■	■	■	■	■	■	■		■	

Additional Varieties:

S3.1.3 Double Painted. Light Blue Over Orange

S3.1.2 The Only Known Lt. Green Example Is Painted Solid Green Inside

S3.1.2 The Only Known Blue Example Is Painted Yellow Inside and Then Over Painted Blue On The Outside

Third or Classic Series Coupes (440 or 330)			Blue-Lt.	Blue	Brown	Camel	Clay	Cream	Flesh	Gray	Green-Forest	Green-Lt.	Green-Moss	Magenta	Orange	Pink	Red	Salmon	Silver	Tan	Yellow	Yellow-Lemon
Plain Coupes																						
CO3.1.1	1939-50s	Cast, Wide Body, Open Wheel-Wells, Unpainted Metal Wheels, Full Grill, Smooth Cast, Wide Body Perhaps '39 Plymouth																				
CO3.1.2	1939	Same as 3.1.1 Except Painted Wheels																				
CO3.1.3	1950s-65	Same as 3.1.1 Except Closed Wheel-Wells																				
CO3.1.4	1957-65	Same as 3.1.3 Except Gold Colored Wheels																				
CO3.1.5	1965	Same as 3.1.3 Except Dull Cleated Rubber Tires																				
Crooked Line Coupe																						
CO3.2.1	1950s-65	Cast, Narrow Body, Closed Wheel-Wells, Metal Wheels, Crooked Line on Right Grill, Tapered Backend Perhaps '37 Willys or '37 Studebaker																				
CO3.2.2	1957-65	Same as 3.2.1 Except Gold Wheels																				
No-Line Coupe																						
CO3.3	1950s-65	Cast, Mid-Width Body, Closed Wheel-Wells, Metal Wheels, Headlight and Three Grill Bars on Left Side, No Headlight and One Grill Bar on Right Side, Later Version had no Headlight or Grill on Left Side, Rounded Backend																				
Additional Variety:																						
CO3.1.3 Double Painted. Light Green Over Pink																						

Fourth or Modern Series Cabs				Blue-Hot	Blue-Dk.	Green-Forest	Orange	Orange-Red Hot	Pink-Hot	Red	Salmon	Yellow-Hot
C 4.1	(BV107a or 107) (330 or 440)	1966-70	Cast, Black Wheels, '63 Ford									
C 4.2	(BV107a or 107) (330 or 440)	1970-71	Cast, Black Wheels with White Sidewalls, '63 Ford									

Fourth or Modern Series Two-Car Trailers					Unpainted
2T4.1	(BV107a)	(330)	1965-70	Same as 2T3.3	
2T4.2	(BV107a)	(330)	1970-71	Same as 2T3.3 with White Sidewalls	

Fourth or Modern Series Four-Car Trailers					Unpainted
4T4.1	(BV107)	(440)	1965-70	Same as 4T3.2.1	
4T4.2	(BV107)	(440)	1965-70	Same as 4T3.2.2	
4T4.3	(BV107)	(440)	1970-71	Same as 4T3.2.1 with White Sidewalls	

Fourth or Modern Series Sedans **(440, 330, or 331)**	**Black**	**Blue**	**Blue-Lt.**	**Flesh**	**Brown-Lt.**	**Chocolate-Metallic**	**Clay**	**Cream**	**Gray**	**Green-Forest**	**Green-Lt.**	**Orange**	**Orange-Hot**	**Pink**	**Pink-Bright**	**Purple**	**Red**	**Silver**	**Tan**	**Yellow**	**Yellow-Lemon**
S4.1.1 1957-65 Cast, Metal Wheels and Axles, Marked 1-8, Open Back Window, Eyelet Axle Holder Perhaps '51 Parkard																					
S4.1.2 1960-65 Same as S4.1.1 Except Gold Wheels																					
S4.2.1.1 1965-66 Same as S4.1.1 Except Cleated Rubber or Plastic Vinyl Tires, Metal Axle made from Pin Crimped at One End, Forked or Eyelet Wheel Assembly, Open Back Window																					
S4.2.1.2 1965-66 Same as S4.2.1.1 Except Closed Back Window																					
S4.2.2.1 1966-70 Same as S4.2.1.1 Except Axle Nub-Both Ends																					
S4.2.2.2 1966-70 Same as S4.2.1.2 Except Axle Nub-Both Ends																					
S4.2.3 1966-70 Same as S4.2.1.2 Except with Small Smooth Rubber Tires, Metal Axle made from Pin Crimped at One End, Forked Axle Holders, Closed Back Window																					

Additional Variety:

S4.1.1 Blue with Painted Tires

S4.3 Fourth or Modern Series Sedans (330, 440, or 331)	Black	Blue	Blue-Metallic	Blue-Hot	Cinnamon-Metallic	Gold	Green-Forest	Green-Metallic	Green-Hot	Maroon	Orange	Orange Hot	Orange-Red Hot	Pink-Hot	Purple-Hot	Red	Red-Hot	Red-Metallic	Silver	Violet	White	Yellow	Yellow-Hot	Yellow-Lemon
S4.3.1 1970-71 Cast, Plastic Wheels, Plastic Axles																								
S4.3.2 1970-71 Same as S4.3.1-Flower Power Label																								
Additional Varieties: Black Over Gold, Black Over Yellow																								

Fourth or Modern Series Coupes (440, 330, or 331)	Aqua	Black	Blue	Blue-Lt.	Blue-Steel	Clay	Gray	Green-Forest	Green-Lt.	Green-Metallic	Gold	Orange	Orange-Burnt	Pink	Pink-Bright	Red	Red-Hot	Salmon	Silver	Tan	Yellow	Yellow-Lemon
CO4.1.1 1957-65 Cast, Metal Wheels and Axles, Marked 1-8, Open Back Window, Eyelet Axle Holder Perhaps '51 Parkard																						
CO4.1.2 1957-65 Same as CO4.1.1 Except Closed Back Window																						
CO4.1.3 1960-65 Same as CO4.1.1 Except Gold Wheels																						
CO4.2.1 1965-66 Same as CO4.1.1 Except Cleated Rubber or Vinyl Plastic Tires, Metal Axle made from Pin Crimped at One End, Forked or Eyelet Wheel Assembly, Closed Back Window																						
CO4.2.2 1966-70 Same as CO4.2.1 Except Axle Nub-Both Ends																						
CO4.2.3 1966-70 Same as CO4.2.1 Except with Small Smooth Rubber Tires, Metal Axle made from Pin Crimped at One End, Forked Axle Holders, Closed Back Window																						

CO4.3 Fourth of Modern Series Coupes **(330, 440, or 331)**	**Black**	**Blue**	**Blue-Metallic**	**Copper**	**Gold**	**Green-Forest**	**Green-Metallic**	**Maroon**	**Orange**	**Orange-Red**	**Orange-Red Hot**	**Pink-Hot**	**Purple-Hot**	**Red**	**Red-Hot**	**Red-Metallic**	**Silver**	**White**	**Yellow**	**Yellow-Hot**
CO4.3 1970-71 Cast, Plastic Wheels, Plastic Axles																				

Endnotes

[1] Stephan, E. A., *O'Brien's Collecting Toy Cars & Trucks 3rd Edition.* Iola, WI: Krause Publications, 2000, 46; and O'Brien, R., *Collecting American-Made Toy Soldiers: Identification and Value Guide 3rd Edition.* Books Americana.

[2] O'Brien, *Soldiers.*

[3] Stephan, 46.

[4] O'Brien, *Soldiers*; and Stephan, E. A., *O'Brien's Collecting Toys 10th Edition*. Iola, WI: Krause Publications, 2001, 610.

[5] O'Brien, *Solders.*

[6] Stephan, *Toy Cars*, 46-57; Stephan, *Collecting Toys*, 610-614. Also, Alekna, "Barclay Car Carriers or Transports, 26-1," *Old Toy Soldier*, 26-29.